LOOKING TO JESUS:
A 30 Day Devotional for Transformation

LOOKING TO JESUS

— A 30 Day Devotional for Transformation —

MIKE AND JODY CLEVELAND

SETTING CAPTIVES FREE
PUBLISHING

Setting Captives Free Publishing
1400 W. Washington St., Ste. 104
Sequim, WA 98382

ISBN: 978-1-7337609-5-9
LCCN: 2019919049

*We dedicate this book to our parents, Ed and Teresa Cleveland
and Dan and Wanda Bryant. Thank you for your
love and support through the years.*

Table of Contents

Acknowledgements

*T*o Rob Robertson, Setting Captives Free Board Member, Supervisor, Brother and Friend:

Thank you for your twenty plus years of friendship and partnership in the gospel. What a blessing and encouragement you are to us! It has been our privilege and pleasure to know you as a precious brother and a dear friend.

We have adapted Paul's words in 1 Thessalonians 1:7-8 to express our appreciation for you: And so, you became a model to all believers everywhere. The Lord's message of the suffering and rising Christ rang out from you not only in Australia but throughout the whole world—your faith in God has become known everywhere.

You are dearly loved for you have made the life and death of Jesus, and His powerful resurrection from the dead, near and dear to our hearts. We are greatly looking forward to the day when we get that great "Aussie bear hug" you've been promising!

Looking to Jesus for Salvation

Just as Moses lifted up the snake in the wilderness, so the Son of Man must be lifted up, that everyone who believes may have eternal life in him..." John 3:14-15

*I*n the beginning, Adam and Eve sinned by turning from God and going their own way of disobedience. From that point on, all people were born dead in our sins and in need of a Savior.

"Therefore, just as sin entered the world through one man, and death through sin, and in this way death came to all people because all sinned..." Romans 5:12

But this was not a surprise to God. God had planned for our need before the foundation of the world (1 Peter 1:18-21). In love, God sent His beloved Son into the world with the name Jesus *"...for he will save his people from their sins."* (Matthew 1:21). And all who believe in Jesus will be saved and given eternal life (John 3:16). Jesus alone is Savior (Acts 4:12).

Before you can experience a real transformation of life, you must first look to Jesus as Savior and be transformed from spiritual death to eternal life (1 John 5:11-12).

"For if, by the trespass of the one man, death reigned through that one man, how much more will those who receive God's abundant provision of grace and of the gift of righteousness reign in life through the one man, Jesus Christ!" Romans 5:17

And what a Savior He is! He is *"...able to save to the uttermost those who draw near to God through Him since He always lives to make intercession for them."* (Hebrews

7:25). No matter what you've done, Jesus is mighty to save you (Isaiah 63:1)!

Oh, friend, look to Jesus, achieving your salvation through His death on the cross. Jesus lived the perfect life you should have lived and then died the death that you deserved so that you might be saved!

On the cross, Jesus took on your sin and gave you His righteousness (2 Corinthians 5:21). Your sins earned death, but Jesus took on your death and overcame it. You sinned and deserved punishment, but Jesus has received all the wrath of God against sin. Jesus took on all your guilt and shame and paid your sin debt so that you are now free to live joyfully and abundantly in a loving relationship with God and others.

When you look to Jesus as Savior, you are seeing what God sees—the atoning blood of His beloved Son. When you put your faith in Jesus as Savior, you are clothed in the righteousness of Christ and acceptable to God (Philippians 3:9, Ephesians 1:5-7).

Illustration

As the Israelites were wandering in the wilderness, they began complaining about their journey. They became angry and resentful toward God and Moses, who was God's representative to them. To correct them, God sent venomous snakes into their camp. The snakes bit the Israelites, and many people died as a result. The rest of the people cried out to God to take the snakes away, and this was God's response:

> *"The Lord said to Moses, "Make a snake and put it up on a pole; anyone who is bitten can look at it and live." So Moses made a bronze snake and put it up on a pole. Then when anyone was bitten by a snake and looked at the bronze snake, they lived." Numbers 21:8-9 (NIV)*

The uplifted snake on a pole was God's method of saving those dying of snakebite. Everyone who looked to the uplifted pole lived.

The serpent of sin has bitten you and me, and we are dying. This snakebite of sin expresses itself in our pride, greed, substance abuse, sexual impurity, uncontrollable rage, unforgiveness, desires for revenge, self-idolatry, etc.

The world and religion would focus you on the problem - the snake bite. The world would teach you to remove the venom through self-help practices; religion teaches you to remove the poison through law-keeping and good works.

But what did God do? He erected a cross-like pole and hung the Savior on it. Jesus Christ and Him crucified is the message of salvation. He hung on the cross so that you can stand unafraid in the judgment. He shed His blood and breathed His last so that you can have life and breath forever. Then Jesus rose from the dead on the third day, having rescued you from sin's trap and death's grip to give you a new and abundant life.

> *"Just as Moses lifted up the snake in the wilderness, so the Son of Man must be lifted up, 15 that everyone who believes may have eternal life in him." John 3:14-15 (NIV)*

Application

Is there some sin that troubles you and causes you to doubt God's love and acceptance of you? Some wrong from your past that haunts your thoughts and worries you? **Look** at Jesus on the cross and **believe** what God tells you about Him. Your sin—past, present, and future—was laid upon Jesus (Isaiah 53:6).

Put your faith in Jesus, and thank God that these sins are no longer on you! Be thankful to Jesus, who bore your sins. Allow Jesus' love to remove your fear and worry (1 John 4:18). Keep looking at Christ on the cross, and Christ, risen from the dead, and walk in the light of God's love and blessing. Jesus has purchased it for you with His precious blood.

Lifted up was He to die; "It is finished!" was His cry; Now in Heav'n exalted high. Hallelujah! What a Savior![1]

Come, friend, be happy in looking to Jesus as your Savior! Enjoy Him. Believe in and focus on Jesus as your Savior and Lord and behold all things shall become new (2 Corinthians 5:17).

---

1   https://library.timelesstruths.org/music/Hallelujah_What_a_Savior/

Question: How does looking to Jesus as Savior give you hope for salvation?

_____

_____

_____

_____

DAY 2:

Looking to Jesus for Transformation

*"And we all, with unveiled face, beholding the glory of
the Lord, are being transformed into the same image
from one degree of glory to another." 2 Corinthians 3:18*

The world teaches us to look at the person in the mirror and "be the change," meaning change your behavior and change your world. They offer programs and self-help books to try to convince you that "you can do it!"

Religion, too, promotes behavior reform and good works as a way to earn favor with God and make the world a better place. Different ideologies but the same approach—they start with the outside, external behavior. But the Bible teaches us that this is not the way to experience transformation.

Jesus explained the futility of the external method of change when He said,

*"For from within, out of the heart of man, come evil thoughts,
sexual immorality, theft, murder, adultery, coveting, wickedness,
deceit, sensuality, envy, slander, pride, foolishness. All these evil
things come from within, and they defile a person." (Mark 7:21-23)*

Here we see that our external behavior is an indication of what is in our hearts. Social and political reform never produces lasting change because these begin with changing externals when what is truly needed is an *internal heart change.*

But we cannot change our hearts. We need *"God, who said, "Let light shine out of darkness,"* to shine in our hearts and give us *"the light of the knowledge of the glory of God in the face of Jesus Christ."* If we want to experience transformation, we must look to the face of One who can change us – Jesus!

Day 2: Looking to Jesus for Transformation

And when we look to Jesus, we see that He has done what we could not. Jesus kept the law perfectly (John 8:29) and then died sacrificially on the cross to atone for our sins (1 John 2:2). At the point of His death on the cross, Jesus became sin so that we might become the righteousness of God (2 Corinthians 5:21). He gave up His Spirit (John 19:30) so that we might receive His Spirit and be filled and transformed from the inside out (Ephesians 1:13-14).

And the beautiful thing about looking to Jesus for transformation is that the moment we look to Jesus in faith, the transformation process begins immediately, and then continues throughout our lives. Immediately, we become a new creation (2 Corinthians 5:17), but continuously, we are transformed into His image as we look to Him (2 Corinthians 3:18).

Illustration

Consider Jesus' own transformation. He was living in radiant glory with the Father, in complete sinless perfection and perfect righteousness. See Him descend from heaven to earth where He took on a human body, and then took on the sins and sickness of the world. He went from blinding glory and spotless righteousness to humiliating shame and sinful wretchedness.

Sin makes us unrecognizable from God's original design for our lives, that of being God's image-bearers; and so Jesus, covered in our sin, was not recognizable either:

> *"Just as there were many who were appalled at him—his appearance was so disfigured beyond that of any human being and his form marred beyond human likeness" Isaiah 52:14 (NIV)*

Look at this shocking transformation Jesus underwent. He, who was the very image of God, righteous and holy, was transformed into your image into your sin. Why? So that you, as a believer in Him, might be transformed into His image, into His righteousness.

Your transformation happens as you hear and believe the transformation message - the death of Jesus for your sins and the resurrection of Jesus from the dead - daily. This message of transformation has the power to profoundly affect our hearts, which is where all real and lasting change begins.

Application

Friend, do you have an area of your life where you want to experience transformation? You can experience the change you desire, but it won't happen by making resolutions, trying to get a handle on your problem, or getting more disciplined in your approach to change.

To be transformed, you must look to Jesus and see His death and resurrection as the foundation for your new life. The more that you behold your Savior in His sufferings and glory, the greater your transformation will be as you enter into the cross/resurrection experience yourself (Romans 6:1-10).

Are you seeking to be pure in heart and mind? Look to Jesus and see how He became filthy with your sin so that you might be made clean. Fill your mind with all that is true and lovely about your Savior, for as you do, you will not gratify the lusts of your flesh.

Are you seeking freedom from gluttony and laziness? Look to Jesus and see how He emptied Himself on the cross, suffering hunger and thirst to provide you with fullness and satisfaction. Look how He laid down His life to purchase the grace that teaches you to say no to your cravings and yes to fellowshipping with Him in His sufferings.

Would you be free from anxiety and depression? Look to your Savior who entered into the darkness and took on all your fears and sorrows and died with them, so that you might have a mind that is sound, a heart full of love, and a new life of power and self-control (2 Timothy 1:7).

Do you want to be free from fear? Fear has to do with punishment, so look to Jesus and see Him punished in your place that you might be pardoned (1 John 4:18), drinking the cup of God's wrath so that there is only love for you.

No matter what the needed change, your transformation begins by looking to Jesus.

Question: How will you look to Jesus for transformation today?

_____

_____

_____

_____

Looking to Jesus for Renewal

"Do not be conformed to this world, but be transformed by the renewal of your mind, that by testing you may discern what is the will of God, what is good and acceptable and perfect." Romans 12:2

Once we come to faith in Christ and begin walking in the Light, we often start to see more clearly how sinful and flawed we are in our flesh. And if we are not careful, we might become confused and distracted and get caught up in trying to renew ourselves through self-effort. We might (perhaps unconsciously) begin a campaign to clean up our act so that we might live free from habitual sin and represent Christ better.

But this is not God's way of renewal for us. Self-effort is the world's way. "Pull yourself up! Do hard things! No pain, no glory!" are the mantras of this world, but Jesus speaks a better word.

When His disciples asked, *"What must we do to be doing the works of God?" Jesus answered them, "This is the work of God, that you believe in him whom he has sent"* (John 6:28-29). The work we do, friend, is to believe in Jesus.

As believers, we must not conform to the world's methods of renewal through self-effort as these are confusing, distracting, and doomed to fail. Instead, we must seek the renewal of our mind through God's Word.

We do not face our problems or sin struggles by tackling them ourselves, turning to laws and rules to change our behavior. Instead, we want to seek transformation by reminding ourselves of what Jesus accomplished for us through His death on the cross and His resurrection from the dead. By meditating on this heart cleansing and mind-renewing message continually and by putting faith in it, a transformation of heart and life is sure.

And this remembering of Jesus' death, and what He accomplished on the cross for us, is not a one-time event nor merely remembering during communion at a church service. No, we must always remind ourselves of the One *"who gave himself for our sins to deliver us from the present evil age…"* (Galatians 1:4; 2 Peter 1:12).

Illustration

In Exodus 14, we read how God rescued the Israelites from slavery in Egypt, and how they were now facing the Red Sea in front of them and Pharoah's pursuing army behind. The Israelites were terrified and trembling; they were murmuring against God and complaining to Moses. They said, *"Was it because there were no graves in Egypt that you brought us to the desert to die? What have you done to us by bringing us out of Egypt?"* (Exodus 14:11).

But in the very next chapter, Exodus 15, we see the Israelites had gone from trembling to worshipping, from complaining to praising.

> *"The Lord is my strength and my defense; he has become my salvation. He is my God, and I will praise him, my father's God, and I will exalt him." Exodus 15:2 (NIV)*

What brought about this renewal of their minds, this great transformation in them, to where they changed from grumbling to praising?

God had rescued and saved them from destruction at the hand of Pharaoh's army and from drowning in the Red Sea.

> *"During the last watch of the night, the Lord looked down from the pillar of fire and cloud at the Egyptian army and threw it into confusion. He jammed the wheels of their chariots so that they had difficulty driving. And the Egyptians said, "Let's get away from the Israelites! The Lord is fighting for them against Egypt." Exodus 14:24-25 (NIV)*

In Exodus 15, the Israelites were reveling in what God had accomplished on their behalf, how He fought for them, how He supernaturally delivered them.

The contemplation of His work on their behalf renewed and transformed them. They went from terror in feeling trapped to fervor in worship, from trembling to praising.

Contemplating how Jesus fought for you on the cross and secured your victory through resurrection power will bring renewal to you too.

Application

Do you want to experience a significant renewal in your mind, life, or behavior?

Hebrews 3 tells you how to receive the help you need: *"Therefore, holy brothers and sisters, who share in the heavenly calling, fix your thoughts on Jesus, whom we acknowledge as our apostle and high priest."* (Hebrews 3:1 NIV)

The way to win the battle against your flesh and to experience the renewal that you want is to fix your thoughts on Jesus.

Remember the agonies of the cross that Jesus endured to cleanse you and heal you. Remember His pierced head, hands, side, and feet, which Jesus displays as He intercedes for you in Heaven. Fill your mind with the truth that you are in Jesus who has risen victorious over death, the world, the devil, and the flesh.

As the song says, *"Would you be free from your passion and pride? There's power in the blood, power in the blood; Come for a cleansing to Calvary's tide; There's wonderful power in the blood."*[2]

As you wash at the "cleansing tide" of the cross and renew your mind in this way, you will experience the Holy Spirit leading you away from ungodly thinking and behavior and into thoughts and actions that are pure, lovely, and of good report. You will not be *trying* to do better; instead, you will be walking by the Spirit and bearing His fruit. Transformation comes not by trying but by dying.

As you fix your thoughts on Jesus, you will begin to live as the new creation He has made you (2 Corinthians 5:17). No longer are you a slave to sin, in bondage to the world and its ideologies; now you are a new creation in Christ Jesus with a mind that is renewed by remembering Christ's death and resurrection and controlled by the love of Jesus who died to save and sanctify you (2 Corinthians 5:14).

2   https://hymnary.org/text/would_you_be_free_from_the_burden_jones

Question: How will you fix your thoughts on Jesus for the renewal of your heart and mind?

_____

_____

_____

_____

Looking to Jesus When Tempted

*"The thief comes only to steal and kill and destroy. I
came that they may have life and have it abundantly."*
John 10:10

Jesus (His life lived perfectly for us, His atoning death, and His victorious resurrection) is the cornerstone of the Christian faith (1 Peter 2:27).
Everything about our faith, everything that is true for us as believers flows
from the finished work of Christ on the cross (John 19:30). Indeed, the message of the cross is the power of God both for unbelievers (Romans 1:16)
and to those who are being saved (1 Corinthians 1:18). When tempted, go
to the cross and look! *"Look, the Lamb of God who takes away the sin of the
world"* (John 1:29).

The death of Jesus is glorious for believers (2 Corinthians 3:8)! His death
saps temptation of its power and brings us transformation and eternal life (John
3:16). With His blood, Jesus has paid our sin debt and removed the curse of the
law and the condemnation that it brought to us (Galatians 3:13-15, Romans 8:1).

Because of our supernatural union with Christ, when He died on the cross,
we died with Him (Romans 6:5). His death was our death (Galatians 2:20). And
our old sinful identities were nailed to a tree in the body of Christ for a very
specific reason. Romans 6:4 explains, *"We were buried therefore with him by
baptism into death, in order that, just as Christ was raised from the dead by the
glory of the Father, we too might walk in newness of life."* Temptation is always
the desire to walk in the old way, to live the old life, but we died with Christ to
the old life, were buried with Him, and were raised from the dead with Him
that we might walk in newness of life.

Oh, friend, do you understand? You had to die with Christ so that you might be raised to abundant living! And this is not merely some future hope or possibility. By faith, you receive your new identity in Christ right now, and you can learn to live today as the new creation that you are in Christ!

And this new life of faith in Jesus is not a drudgery or something to be endured. No! Your new life in Christ is one of joy amid sorrow, peace in times of uncertainty, strength in times of weakness, and abundance in moments of need. It is a life not driven by the cravings of your flesh, the allurement of the world, or the deceitfulness of Satan. Your new life is guided by the Holy Spirit (Romans 8:14).

But this new and abundant life does not come naturally to us. We must learn how to live it. The apostle Paul wrote, *"I press on to take hold of that for which Christ Jesus took hold of me. Brothers and sisters, I do not consider myself yet to have taken hold of it. But one thing I do: Forgetting what is behind and straining toward what is ahead, I press on toward the goal to win the prize for which God has called me heavenward in Christ Jesus."* (Philippians 3:12-14 NIV).

If you want to experience the abundant life that Jesus died to give you, you must forget what is behind and press on toward experiencing Christ. You do this by fixing your thoughts on Him (Hebrews 3:1), fixing your eyes on Him (Hebrews 12:2), remembering His death and rejoicing in His resurrection.

The evil one will tempt you, trying to remind you of your sinful past, to entice you to return to it. Your flesh will call you to return to your old sinful ways of eating, drinking, and living. The world will entice you to conform to their version of the abundant life full of stuff, trinkets, and shiny things, but remember, you are dead to the world, dead to your past and alive in Christ. Look to and believe in Jesus, and *"rivers of living water"* will flow to and through you (John 7:38).

Illustration

> *"The rabble with them began to crave other food, and again the Israelites started wailing and said, "If only we had meat to eat! We remember the fish we ate in Egypt at no cost—also the cucumbers, melons, leeks, onions, and garlic. But now we have lost our appetite; we never see anything but this manna!" Numbers 11:4-6 (NIV)*

At this point in their journey, the Israelites had been out of Egypt for over two years. They were no longer slaves; they were God's chosen people. And as God's chosen people, they had repeatedly watched as God protected them and provided for their needs.

Nevertheless, when faced with day after day of hot, barren desert, they wearied and began to complain. Instead of remembering all that God had done for them, they recalled the good food they ate while in slavery, and this led them to a place of sorrow, discontent, and frustration.

Oh, friend, this happens to us too. The world calls us to return to it, reminding us of the pleasure we had in indulging our flesh and promising *"abundant life"* if we will but return to it. Our flesh wearies of Jesus, the spiritual Bread (John 6:48-51), and longs for the physical, the immediate, the natural, and the carnal. But we must not believe the lies of the world, the devil, or our flesh. Only Christ can satisfy your hungry heart. Only Christ provides abundant life to you because He suffered death in your place.

Application

When you are enticed to return to fleshly living, look at the cross! Remind yourself that you died to sin, you died to fleshly living, you died to Satan's *"cucumbers, melons, leeks, onions, and garlic."* Remind yourself that Jesus rose out of the grave of death and that you rose out of the grave of fleshly living. Put your back toward Egypt and continue to behold the Lamb of God, who took away your sin!

Are you trapped by sin or stuck in the ways, thoughts, or reactions of your old life? There is hope for you in Jesus. Look to Him as your Good Shepherd, who laid down His life to save you. See Him being devoured by the wolves of sin, death, and hell to spare you. Believe the good news that Jesus has defeated your enemies! Now, see Him risen, scarred but completely whole, and full of life calling to you to follow Him to places of rest and refreshment. Call to Him; He will set you free.

Are you weary of life? Have you pursued satisfaction and fulfillment in your spouse, children, job, or possessions only to find yourself disappointed and disillusioned? Come to Jesus, the Giver of abundant life (John 10:10, Psalm 34:4). His mercy and grace are new every morning (Lamentations 3:23). His faithfulness is great when yours isn't (Psalm 36:5). You have looked for life, love, and satisfaction in temporary things, but Christ's righteousness overcomes your failings (1 Corinthians 1:26-31). Look to His cross and see that He has abandoned His own life to make yours abundant. Now, see the empty tomb, believe that Your Savior is risen and rejoice because Christ lives in You (Galatians 2:20)!

No temptation has overtaken you except what is common to mankind. And God is faithful; he will not let you be tempted beyond what you can bear. But when you are tempted, he will also provide a way out so that you can endure it. 1 Corinthians 10:13 NIV

Question: How can you look to Jesus as your way out of temptation today?

_____

_____

_____

_____

Looking to Jesus When Habitually Sinning

"So you also must consider yourselves dead to sin and alive to God in Christ Jesus." Romans 6:11

We all have sin that easily entangles us (Hebrews 12:1), but as believers, we don't want to live in sin. We want to be mastered by Christ, not our sin (Romans 6:14). But this begs the question, how can we throw off the sins that hinder us in our daily walk? How can we overcome sins that we've dealt with for much of our lives?

In Romans 6, we find that our death with Christ means freedom from the power of sin. God established a union between believers and Christ (1 Corinthians 1:30) so that God counts Christ's death on the cross as our death. If we would lay aside the sin that frustrates us, we must believe ourselves dead to it. We must see ourselves hanging on the cross with Jesus and buried in the tomb with Jesus. That is, our old person, our old self, died on the cross and was buried. Now we respond to sin's temptations differently, for we consider ourselves dead to sin and alive to God.

When we die physically, our bodies become unresponsive to stimuli. Likewise, because of our union with Christ in His death and resurrection, we consider ourselves dead to sin and unresponsive to it. Picture yourself in a casket, and then see someone laying temptations to sin all around that casket; how would you respond? Dead people do not respond to stimuli. *"So you also must consider yourselves dead to sin and alive to God in Christ Jesus." Romans 6:11*

This is what we are demonstrating when we submit to water baptism; we go under the water as a symbol of being buried with Christ. Burial is for the dead. Our old self died, our old identity died, our old labels died, our old way of living died! And we rise a new creation, united with Christ in all of life.

And while death is usually considered a sad thing, for us who believe, our spiritual death is a happy event because it means we are now hidden in Christ (Colossians 3:3). Our death in Christ means safety and sanctification for us. It means that the world, the flesh, and the devil have no claim on our hearts, minds, or bodies. We are no longer living in sin; we are dead to sin. We are dead to the world's allurements. We are dead to our past life. We are dead to old labels that were placed on us. This is the wonderfully good news of the beautiful, terrible cross: we died with Christ!

> *May I never boast except in the cross of our Lord Jesus Christ, through which the world has been crucified to me, and I to the world. Galatians 6:14 (NIV)*

Illustration

The Israelites were set free from slavery through the death of the Passover Lamb, but then they immediately came to the Red Sea. As God performed a miracle and parted the sea for them, they walked through on dry ground, a wall of water on the left and the right.

Notice what the Israelites passing through the Red Sea is called in the New Testament:

> *"For I do not want you to be ignorant of the fact, brothers and sisters, that our ancestors were all under the cloud and that they all passed through the sea. They were all baptized into Moses in the cloud and in the sea." 1 Corinthians 10:1-2 (NIV)*

Yes, baptism! The fact that the Israelites were "baptized" as they passed through the Red sea meant, for them, that they died to their old life of slavery. And when they rose out of the waters on the other side, they entered into a new life of freedom. They died to their old identity, their old life, their entire past. Not only did the Passover Lamb die for them, they, themselves, "died" and "rose" again. They would no longer see themselves as slaves but as God's children. They would no longer have a harsh taskmaster over them; they were free!

At the cross, you died to your old life of slavery and rose with Jesus to a new life of freedom. See yourself dead to sin and your past life, dear friend, for that is where the freedom is. Now, see yourselves alive to God, responsive to Him, walking with Him daily.

> *"For we know that our old self was crucified with him so that the body ruled by sin might be done away with, that we should no longer be slaves to sin — because anyone who has died has been set free from sin." Romans 6:6-7 (NIV)*

Application

Oh, friend, your death with Christ is such good news! When sin comes knocking on your heart's door, you are no longer obligated to answer, because you are dead to it. You have died with Christ on His cross; you have been buried with Him in the tomb. You have been raised with Him to a new life!

Are you struggling with greed—wanting more, more, more? Come to the cross of Christ and see yourself as dying with Him. See yourself giving up your spirit so that you might be filled with the Spirit of the Living God who satisfies with good things (Psalm 103:5).

Are you struggling with overwhelming sorrow? Come to Christ and see that He carried your sorrows in His body on the tree (Isaiah 53:4). You and your grief died with Christ, so you no longer grieve as those who have no hope (1 Thessalonians 4:13). You are united with the One who brings life and renewal to places that were once defined by darkness and death (Isaiah 58:11). Come and live in the light of His presence (Psalm 89:15, Ephesians 4:8) so that your joy will be restored (Psalm 51:12).

Does your flesh trouble you and clamor to be gratified? Run to the cross of Christ, friend, look up, and see your flesh united to the Lamb of God wounded and dying and then dead. Watch as they bury Christ and your flesh with Him in the tomb. Do you see it? Your body of death is dead! Through His death and resurrection, Jesus has delivered you (Romans 7:24-25)! You are free from sin's penalty through Jesus' death on the cross and are being freed from sin's power

(Romans 6:7). You have risen with Christ to a new life, and God has given you saving grace that teaches you "to renounce ungodliness and worldly passions, and to live self-controlled, upright, and godly lives…" today!

Yes, we can still be tempted, even Jesus was tempted in every way that we are. But, you can consider yourself dead to sin because God has united you with Christ in His death. *"Let not sin therefore reign in your mortal body, to make you obey its passions. Do not present your members to sin as instruments for unrighteousness, but present yourselves to God as those who have been brought from death to life, and your members to God as instruments for righteousness."* Romans 6:12-13

> **Question:** How does looking to Jesus and His cross, help you see yourself as dead to sin?
>
> _____
>
> _____
>
> _____
>
> _____

Looking to Jesus When Burdened by Guilt

"Now it is evident that no one is justified before God by the law, for 'The righteous shall live by faith.'" Galatians 3:11

D o you ever struggle with guilt over sins you've committed or your failure to do what is right? Have you felt shame related to your past or present? Does your inability to "measure up" depress you? Many Christians wrestle with these types of feelings.

These thoughts of guilt, shame, and failure can make us feel like a hostage, trapped in a vicious cycle of sin and shame that frustrates and discourages. If this is you today, Jesus invites you to look to Him for relief from your burden of guilt.

When sin entered our world, the burden of guilt and shame came in like a flood (Genesis 3:6-10). No amount of good works or right behavior on man's part could make things right again, but God devised a way for us (2 Samuel 14:14, John 14:6) through His Son Jesus (John 3:16, Romans 5:19).

If you put your faith in Jesus then God declares you, "Not guilty!" based on what Christ did for you through His perfect life, atoning death and triumphant resurrection (Romans 4:25, Romans 5:9). You are justified by grace (Titus 3:7; Romans 4:2–5), through faith (Acts 13:39; Romans 5:1), because of Jesus (Romans 5:16; Galatians 2:16–17).

As your representative, Jesus lived perfectly—never sinning, always doing the will of the Father, never falling short, continuously measuring up. And by grace, Jesus' perfect life has been credited to you. Jesus has earned eternal life and acceptance for you. When God looks at you, He sees the perfect righteousness that Jesus has given to you. You are not guilty, Jesus took that burden on Himself for you; now you are righteous because God has declared it so (2 Corinthians 5:21).

When Jesus died on the cross, He took on all your sins (past, present, and future). Those sins are no longer yours; He has taken them from you so that you can be free from them and the guilt and shame that came with them (1 Peter 2:24). Now, there is no condemnation for you because Jesus was condemned in your place! (Romans 8:1). There is no punishment for you because Jesus has taken it on your behalf (Isaiah 53:5). You are free from your burden of guilt and free to live a life of joy in Jesus!

Illustration

In the Book of Philemon, we read about a slave by the name of Onesimus who stole money from his master, Philemon, and then ran away. But apparently, Onesimus ran right into the Apostle Paul who was a friend of Philemon. Paul shared the message of Jesus' death and resurrection with Onesimus, and by grace, Onesimus became a believer in Jesus. Paul then wrote a letter and sent Onesimus back to his master, Philemon, with it.

Onesimus was guilty under the law. Onesimus owed a debt to Philemon. With this in mind, Paul writes to Philemon (the master) about Onesimus (his former slave):

> "Formerly he was useless to you, but now he has become useful both to you and to me. I am sending him—who is my very heart—back to you. So if you consider me a partner, welcome him as you would welcome me. If he has done you any wrong or owes you anything, charge it to me. I, Paul, am writing this with my own hand. I will pay it back." Philemon 1:11-12, 18-19 (NIV)

The Apostle Paul was willing to pay the debt of another! To relieve Onesimmus of his burden! What kind of love must Paul have had for Onesimus to take Onesimus' burden and carry it? To assume his debt and pay it? A very strong love, indeed Paul called him "my very heart." Because of Paul's intercession and willingness to assume the debt, Onesimus came home to Philemon free of all charges, as if he had never stolen, and was accepted as if he were the Apostle

Paul himself! He was received as a beloved brother now, not a mere slave.

Such is the same kind of love that Jesus has for you! You, like Onesimus, have done wrong, and have become guilty before a holy God. You owed a great debt to God. This debt could only be paid by death, for *the wages of sin is death* (Romans 6:23). But hear these words to you today, the words that Jesus says to the Father on your behalf:

> *The debt he/she owes to You, and any wrongs done, have been charged to my account. I, Jesus, am writing this with my own nail-pierced hand, I have paid it back. I am sending this one, who is my very heart, back to You. He/she is not guilty, and I'm thankful that You receive them as you would receive Me.*

Jesus Christ assumed your guilt and paid off your debt of sin. Look at Him dying on the cross as a guilty Man, and understand that your guilt was removed, your debt paid, and your pardon purchased!

Application

Next time feelings of guilt and shame burden you, look to Jesus and His cross to see that your sins have been removed from you and paid for by Jesus. Wash away your guilt and shame in the blood of the Lamb. You have been justified and declared righteous by God because of Jesus. By grace, Jesus has set you free from the guilt of your sin.

When the fear of God's anger floods your mind, and you imagine that you are so terrible there is no way that God could forgive you, look to the cross and see your gruesome sin hanging there in the body of Christ receiving the punishment you deserve. And then hear Jesus yell out in a loud voice, "It is finished!" meaning "Paid in Full!" Your sin debt has been erased, friend. "Shake off your guilty fears."[3] The Father has received "the bleeding sacrifice" of Jesus in your place, and pardoned you because of Him.

Jesus' wounds plead for your forgiveness. Through His death and resurrection, Jesus has justified you! You have nothing to fear because you are in

---

3   http://hymnbook.igracemusic.com/hymns/arise-my-soul-arise

Christ. Receive the love of God as it flows from the cross of Christ and let it cast out all your fear so that you can move forward in faith!

And to the one who does not work but believes in him who justifies the ungodly, his faith is counted as righteousness. (Romans 4:5)

Question: How does looking to Jesus and believing in Him relieve you of the burden of guilt?

_____

_____

_____

_____

Looking to Jesus When Feeling Unloved

"...instead the Lord your God turned the curse into a blessing for you, because the Lord your God loved you."
Deuteronomy 23:5

Feeling unloved or unwanted is a common struggle in our world. Increasing rates of suicide, divorce, and substance abuse prove it. And while many varying factors can foster the belief that we are unloved, we will see that the primary origin of this lie is our own hearts.

To a world that turned away from God to look for love in all the wrong places, God came in a human body. He came because He so loved the world (John 3:16). He came to demonstrate His love through a Sacrifice.

In the Person of Jesus Christ, God loved you and gave Himself for you (Galatians 2:20). This sacrifice was so bold and so powerful that through it, God saved the world, and at the same time, through that same sacrifice, God loved our hearts and taught us how to live. *"This is how we know what love is: Jesus Christ laid down his life for us. And we ought to lay down our lives for our brothers and sisters"* (1 John 3:16).

People have been longing for love and acceptance since the beginning of time. But this is not only due to poor parenting, abuse, or abandonment from our past; it is primarily due to hearts damaged by sin, which can only be healed by our Savior.

Illustration

In Genesis 2 and 3, we read that God created Adam and Eve to enjoy a loving relationship with Himself and with each other. But when sin entered the world, there was a dark shift.

Notice Adam's behavior after his sin,

> *"And they heard the sound of the Lord God walking in the garden in the cool of the day, and the man and his wife hid themselves from the presence of the Lord God among the trees of the garden. But the Lord God called to the man and said to him, "Where are you?" And he said, "I heard the sound of you in the garden, and I was afraid because I was naked, and I hid myself." He said, "Who told you that you were naked? Have you eaten of the tree of which I commanded you not to eat?" The man said, "The woman whom you gave to be with me, she gave me fruit of the tree, and I ate." (Genesis 3:8-12).*

Before sin, Adam and Eve happily met with God in loving fellowship, but after sin, they hid from God out of fear and shame. Instead of cherishing his God-given helper, sin motivated Adam to distance himself from Eve and cast blame on her. Adam's sin affected him so much that he became actively opposed to his wife. Adam said to God, "The woman...she gave me fruit of the tree, and I ate." Adam blamed Eve for his own failure. Adam did not say, "my wife, my loving wife," but rather, "this woman." Sin divides the most united hearts and ruins the most blessed unions.

Sin distorted and confused Adam. Before sin, Adam believed that he was loved and wanted by God and by Eve, but after his encounter with sin, Adam felt differently. He no longer felt acceptable as he was; he thought he needed to do something to "cover" himself. He hid from God and pushed away Eve. Love was displaced by fear.

Friend, sin does this to us too. We have all sinned, and so, we all go through times where we feel unloved, unwanted, unacceptable. But there is a remedy for our wounded hearts and minds, and it is the same remedy that God presented to Adam thousands of years ago.

"And the Lord God made for Adam and for his wife garments of skins and clothed them." Genesis 3:21

God never stopped loving or wanting Adam and Eve, but their sin was a barrier in their relationships. Adam and Eve could not remove the barrier, so God did. God made a sacrifice on Adam and Eve's behalf so that they could be clothed. The covering of the sacrifice restored their fellowship with God and each other. It restored love in their hearts and their union together.

That first sacrifice by God pointed forward to the ultimate sacrifice that Jesus would make on the cross to demonstrate His eternal love for us (1 John 4:10). The cross is where we see that we are fully and forever loved 1 John 4:16)!

Friend, you are loved! Because of Jesus' death on the cross, if you put your faith in Him, you can say, *"I will greatly rejoice in the Lord; my soul shall exult in my God, for he has clothed me with the garments of salvation; he has covered me with the robe of righteousness,"* (Isaiah 61:10).

Application

When your heart is heavy and weighed down with thoughts that you are unloved, look to the cross of Christ and see that God loves you so much that He sacrificed His own Son to demonstrate His love for you (Romans 5:8). Speak to your heart of the immeasurable love of God that spared nothing to save you and from which nothing can separate you (Romans 8:32-38). As you look to the cross, you can say with Paul that Jesus *"loved me and gave Himself for me"* (Galatians 2:20).

If other people reject you or make you feel unloved, remember Jesus, who endured the rejection of all, even His own Father, so that you might always be accepted (Psalm 27:10, Isaiah 53:3, Luke 9:22, Mark 15:34, Romans 15:7). Your value is not determined by another person but by Christ who died on a terrible cross, rose again, and now intercedes for you.

Other humans will disappoint, hurt, forget, and fail you, but God never will (Isaiah 49:15). He has proven His love for you; you are in His forever family—loved and wanted (Romans 5:8, 1 John 3:1).

If you ever feel unloved or unwanted, look at the cross and see Jesus taking your curse and turning it into a blessing for you (Galatians 3:13-14) because

He loves you. *"…instead the Lord your God turned the curse into a blessing for you, because the Lord your God loved you." Deuteronomy 23:5*

"Greater love has no one than this, that someone lay down his life for his friends." John 15:13

Question: How does the cross of Christ demonstrate that you are deeply and forever loved and wanted?

_____

_____

_____

_____

Looking to Jesus When Surrounded by Turmoil

Peace I leave with you; my peace I give you. I do not give to you as the world gives. Do not let your hearts be troubled and do not be afraid. John 14:27

*M*ass shootings, natural disasters, political unrest, and financial market instability dominate the news of today. Fallen pastors and false teachers abound. Our daily lives, too, are frequently fraught with trauma, unexpected difficulties, or unwanted intrusions. All this can, at times, cause our hearts to falter and trouble us with fear, worry, and anxiety. What are we to do when our hearts are in turmoil?

Colossians 3:15 guides us, *"And let the peace of Christ rule in your hearts, to which indeed you were called in one body. And be thankful."*

Friend, in your world of trouble, Jesus invites you today to look to Him for peace. And this is not a temporary or a mere pretense of peace like the world offers, Jesus gives a heart mending, mind-calming, beyond comprehension kind of peace that is effective for today and forever.

Look to Jesus and remember that you were once alienated from God, dead in your sins, living in darkness and rebellion, but in love, Christ died for you. Through Jesus' finished work on the cross, He brought peace to you (Romans 5:1-8). On the cross, He purchased your peace.

Because Jesus opened a new and living way through His death (Hebrews 10:20), you can enjoy an intimate and eternal relationship with God (James 4:8) and, because Jesus has torn down the wall of hostility, you can have, as much as possible, peaceful relationships with others (Romans 12:18, Ephesians 2:14).

As God's child, when feeling turmoil within, you have a safe place to run where you can cast all your cares (1 Peter 5:7). You can look to Jesus on the cross and experience the love that casts out all fear and the peace that passes all understanding today because your eternal life is secure in Christ (1 John 4:18, Philippians 4:7). You can live by faith because you have hope in Jesus and His death and resurrection (Hebrews 6:19, 2 Corinthians 5:7). Because you have been saved forever, you can live confident that today, God will keep you through the storms of life (Psalm 27:5, Luke 8:23).

Illustration

When Jesus died on the cross, His followers were confused and downcast; their hearts were in turmoil because they did not yet understand what God was doing. They didn't understand that the suffering of Jesus was purchasing their eternal life and their freedom from turmoil. But days later, the risen Christ came to His disciples with His peace.

> *On the evening of that day, the first day of the week, the doors being locked where the disciples were for fear of the Jews, Jesus came and stood among them and said to them, "Peace be with you." When he had said this, he showed them his hands and his side. Then the disciples were glad when they saw the Lord. Jesus said to them again, "Peace be with you. As the Father has sent me, even so, I am sending you." And when he had said this, he breathed on them and said to them, "Receive the Holy Spirit. If you forgive the sins of any, they are forgiven them; if you withhold forgiveness from any, it is withheld." John 20:19-23*

Do you see how Jesus connects the disciple's peace with His wounds? *"Peace be with you. When he had said this, He showed them His hands and His side."* Friend, look at the wounds of Jesus, remember the cross of Jesus, and be at peace. For Jesus has removed your sin (John 1:29), redeemed you from the curse of the Law (Galatians 3:13-14), justified you before God (Romans 4:25), nailed to the cross the legal document of your wrongs (Colossians 2:14), and bought your eternal life (John 3:16).

Application

As believers, we have the choice of letting the peace of Christ rule in our hearts or being dominated by fear and worry. Fear and anxiety bring sleepless nights, poor health, and unstable emotions, but the peace of Christ fosters a sound mind and spirit that is thankful and at rest regardless of the storm that rages (2 Timothy 1:7).

When doubts and fears surface or calamity strikes, and our hearts are in turmoil, we need only look to Jesus for His peace. As we look to the cross of Christ and remember that Jesus has made peace with God for us, we can trust Him to bring peace to the various situations in our lives.

Are you hurting because of broken relationships? Look to Jesus and see that He is the great Reconciler. He has reconciled you to the eternal God through His death and resurrection. He can bring healing to your temporary relationships if that's His will or give you peace and acceptance if it isn't (Matthew 12:50, 1 Peter 3:8, Colossians 3:13).

Are you frightened or anxious about the uncertain circumstances of your world? Look to Jesus and believe in Him who, as God and man, fought your fight and won it, accepted your sin debt and paid it, took your sins and died under them, and rose again to set you free to a new life of peace and power in Him. He will never leave or forsake you (Hebrews 13:5)! He has secured your life today and forever (John 3:16). As you set your mind on things above, these temporary troubles will cease to torment your mind, you will have peace, and you will be ready to speak of the hope that is within you (Colossians 3:2, 1 Peter 1:13-16).

> *"You keep him in perfect peace whose mind is stayed on you because he trusts in you." Isaiah 26:3*

Question: How does looking to Jesus bring peace to your heart and mind today?

_____

_____

_____

Looking to Jesus When Feeling Sad

*"For you, O Lord, have made me glad by your work; at
the works of your hands, I sing for joy." Psalm 92:4*

Thousands of years ago, King Solomon, observed, *"I perceived that there is nothing better for them than to be joyful and to do good as long as they live…"* (Ecclesiastes 3:12) Still today, we sing songs about happiness and take trips (physically and mentally) to our happy places. We look for joy in nature, each other, and various activities. Indeed, the pursuit of happiness is considered by many to be a natural God-given right.

But how do we know happiness when our circumstances are dark, and we feel sad? What do we do when we get the word that someone we love has died, our business has failed, our relationship is fractured, or our body is diseased?

At a very difficult time in his life and ministry, Paul wrote, *"Therefore we do not lose heart. Though outwardly we are wasting away, yet inwardly we are being renewed day by day. For our light and momentary troubles are achieving for us an eternal glory that far outweighs them all. So we fix our eyes not on what is seen, but on what is unseen, since what is seen is temporary, but what is unseen is eternal."* (2 Corinthians 4:16-18). And he gave the reason for his courage and hope amid difficult circumstances in 2 Corinthians 4:14, *"because we know that the one who raised the Lord Jesus from the dead will also raise us with Jesus and present us with you to himself."*

Friend, circumstances are not always happy, but when you know "the One who raised the Lord Jesus from the dead," you can have never-ending joy. Jesus has worked mightily for you on the cross, dear friend, and He is even now interceding for you before the throne of God. For this reason, you can look to

Him and sing with joy whether your cupboards are full (Psalm 65:11), or you are facing the fight of your life (1 Timothy 6:12-13).

Illustration

The Bible tells us about a man named Stephen, who was *"full of faith and the Holy Spirit"* (Acts 6:5), as he was always looking at Jesus. *"All who were sitting in the Sanhedrin looked intently at Stephen, and they saw that his face was like the face of an angel"* (Acts 6:15). He gave out the message of Jesus Christ and Him crucified (Acts 6:52), and this brought joy to his heart, amid the persecution of his life.

For his preaching the death and resurrection of Christ, Stephen was stoned. But notice how God sustained Stephen and gave him joy through this terrible ordeal that ended in his death:

> *"When the members of the Sanhedrin heard this, they were furious and gnashed their teeth at him. But Stephen, full of the Holy Spirit, looked up to heaven and saw the glory of God, and Jesus standing at the right hand of God. "Look," he said, "I see heaven open and the Son of Man standing at the right hand of God." Acts 7:54-56 (NIV)*

What did Stephen see as he was being stoned? He saw Jesus standing at the right hand of God! Jesus, though always seated at the right hand of the Father (Hebrews 10:12), rose to greet Stephen. And in seeing Jesus, Stephen saw heaven opened (as did John Revelation 19:11). Stephen understood the secret to having joy in hostile circumstances – looking to Jesus.

At the cross, Jesus offered Himself as your sacrifice, and as He did, the temple veil into the Most Holy place was torn in two from top to bottom. Jesus opened up a new and living way for you to come into the presence of God clothed in His sacrifice (Hebrews 10:20). Now, you can boldly come before the throne of God, and like Stephen receive sustaining grace that produces joy in your heart and enables you to sing through the painful and frightening moments of life (Hebrews 4:16, Acts 16:25).

Stephen's tormentors hurled stones at him, but he did not focus on his persecutors or the rocks that they threw. Stephen looked at Jesus and had joy, which radiated on his face (Acts 6:15). He bravely faced death because He was looking to Jesus who had overcome death for him. Sadness cannot prevail and is replaced with joy when looking at Jesus.

Application

Are you feeling heavy in your heart, mourning the loss of a loved one, a relationship, or your health? Are you full of sadness? Look to Jesus and remember that He was engulfed in darkness on the cross, forsaken for you so that you would be raised to walk in the light of His love and presence (John 8:12, 1 John 1:7). He has borne your sicknesses and carried your sorrows so that you would not be overcome (Isaiah 53:4-5) by them. Come to the cross, believe in Jesus, and *"rejoice with joy that is inexpressible and filled with glory, obtaining the outcome of your faith, the salvation of your souls."* (1 Peter 1:8-9).

Are you looking for happiness in temporary things? Have you looked for joy in your job or hobbies, your spouse, children, church, or friends only to be disappointed again and again? Have you drunk of sparkling wine (or food, sexual impurity, etc.), thinking it would bring you happiness only to wake up with bitter regret (Proverbs 23:31-32)? Look to Jesus and see that He drank the bitter cup of God's wrath, suffered utter disappointment, gave up everything, was abandoned by everyone on the cross so that He could give you fullness of joy and eternal happiness (Psalm 16:11). Come to Him, sit at His feet, delight in Him; Jesus satisfies. He is the One that you want and need.

> *"You make known to me the path of life; in your presence, there is fullness of joy; at your right hand are pleasures forevermore."*
> *Psalm 16:11*

Question: How does looking to Jesus' death and resurrection bring joy to your heart today?

_____

_____

_____

DAY 10:

Looking to Jesus for Acceptance

*"By faith Abel offered to God a more acceptable sacri-
fice than Cain, through which he was commended as
righteous, God commending him by accepting his gifts.
And through his faith, though he died, he still speaks."*
Hebrews 11:4

From infancy, we all want to be accepted. Little ones often mimic the behaviors of those who care for them in an attempt to gain attention and affection, desiring to be accepted. Older children and teens might try to please parents, teachers, or friends by saying or doing whatever gains them approval. Some of us get so caught up in the pursuit of love and acceptance that we find ourselves doing things that we regret.

The sad thing is that in the end, we discover that social acceptance doesn't fully satisfy us. It's temporary and inadequate. What we really want; what we so desperately need is acceptance from God. The only problem is that we know we aren't acceptable. The attitudes in our hearts and frequently our actions, too, evidence that we have rejected God's ways, and our human logic tells us that for this, we deserve God's rejection. What are we to do?

And because of our great need and God's immeasurable love, He sent Jesus. *"For our sake he made him to be sin who knew no sin, so that in him we might become the righteousness of God." 2 Corinthians 5:21* The great exchange of the gospel is that Jesus suffered the consequences of our sins so that we might receive His righteousness before God. Righteousness means you are right with God; you are accepted. It means that now, when God looks at you, He is pleased with you.

Illustration

In Genesis 4, we learn that two sons were born to Adam and Eve; their names were Cain and Abel. These brothers had no doubt heard from their parents that to approach a holy God, in their sinful state, required a sacrifice. But the kinds of sacrifices these brothers brought teach us much about how we, ourselves, are accepted by God.

> *"In the course of time, Cain brought some of the fruits of the soil as an offering to the Lord. 4 And Abel also brought an offering—fat portions from some of the firstborn of his flock. The Lord looked with favor on Abel and his offering, but on Cain and his offering he did not look with favor. So Cain was very angry, and his face was downcast." Genesis 4:3-5 (NIV)*

Cain brought "some of the fruits of the soil." He was a hard worker in his fields, he planted and harvested, and from his labors, he brought God an offering. Cain thought the fruit of his hard work merited God's acceptance.

Abel, on the other hand, brought a sacrifice of blood, an offering from his flock that he had killed. Abel understood, probably from the sacrifice that God made for his parents (Genesis 3:21), the depths of his sin, and the requirement for blood to be shed for forgiveness. Abel evidenced that he understood what would later be said clearly in Hebrews 9:22 *"In fact, the law requires that nearly everything be cleansed with blood, and without the shedding of blood there is no forgiveness."*

And who received God's favor? *"The Lord looked with favor on Abel and his offering."* The Lord accepted Abel because the Lord accepted Abel's offering. There was blood in that offering, which pointed forward to the blood Jesus would shed on the cross to forgive all who come to God through Him. Abel was accepted because of his sacrifice, and you and I are accepted because of the sacrifice of Jesus Christ in our place, for our sins, as our Substitute.

Application

Jesus sacrificed Himself on the cross so that when God looks at you through the blood of Jesus, you are seen as perfect. God loves and accepts you! Because you are in Christ, because you are one with Christ, you eternally hear, *"This is my Son (or daughter), whom I love; with him/her, I am well pleased." (Matthew 3:17).*

Have you been working hard to earn God's favor? Do you struggle with feeling unacceptable to God or think that you must obey all the rules to stay in God's good graces? Look to Jesus and see that He took on all your sins on the cross, and in exchange, He gave you His perfect, God-pleasing righteousness. His perfection has been gifted to you. You didn't get a second chance to obey the law; you received the righteousness of Christ. God cannot reject you because *you are in Christ.* Your sin debt has been paid. God knows you fully and loves you eternally!

Are you a people pleaser? Would you like to be liberated from living for human acceptance? Look to Jesus on the cross, who took the rejection of everyone, so that you could receive eternal acceptance from the only One that truly matters - God! You are loved and accepted in Jesus, dear friend. Turn from seeking the approval of man, and instead, walk in the smile of Your God and enjoy the light of His love.

> *"having predestined us to adoption as sons by Jesus Christ to Himself, according to the good pleasure of His will, to the praise of the glory of His grace, by which He made us **accepted in the Beloved**. In Him, we have redemption through His blood, the forgiveness of sins, according to the riches of His grace."* Ephesians 1:5-7

Question: How does looking to Jesus assure you that you are accepted by God?

Looking to Jesus When Struggling with Bitterness

"See to it that no one fails to obtain the grace of God; that no "root of bitterness" springs up and causes trouble, and by it many become defiled;" Hebrews 12:15

e have all tasted the bitter waters of life in some way. Violations, injustice, false accusations, abuse, and a myriad of other offenses wound us and produce pain in our lives. No one escapes betrayal.

Some respond to the betrayals of life by hiding their pain, pretending they are immune to it. They bury their pain deep down, not realizing that eventually, it will erupt out of them in a bitter, destructive, and defiling way. Others broadcast their betrayal; they talk about it to anyone who will listen. These are at high risk for bitterness because they are always thinking about and reliving their injury. A few will immediately respond in bitterness by seeking revenge, desiring to inflict as much pain as they have felt on their offender, and more if possible.

Bitterness is what happens when we remember the offenses against us but forget the gospel that is for us. We relive the hurts; we dwell on the events, we replay the offense(s). As believers in Jesus, God has given us a way to process our pain and anger without sinning. We have a heavenly hospital to which we can come, have our pain addressed, and receive healing. This place is the cross of Christ.

It is true. The place of Christ's ultimate betrayal is where we find our complete healing. When we experience the pain of betrayal, we can find relief through the cross of Christ. We look to Jesus and His cross and see that God is a God of justice. He does not ignore sin. He crucified it. He sent His Son to endure the agony of affliction, the full weight of every sin and offense, so that not only would we be justified before Him but also that we would be assured of justice for ourselves. Jesus' death pays not only for your sinful offenses but also for the offenses of others against you. He died on the cross and rose to bring healing, reconciliation, and restoration to our lives.

Illustration

As the Israelites traveled through the desert on their way to the Promised Land, they went through many barren places. At one point in their journey, after three days without finding any water, they came to an area with water only to discover that the water was bitter. *"When they came to Marah, they could not drink its water because it was bitter" (Exodus 15:23).*

By this time, the people were very thirsty and distressed, and when they found the bitter water, they reacted badly. They grumbled to Moses, who then cried out to the Lord for help. God answered with an unusual solution:

> *"Then Moses cried out to the Lord, and the Lord showed him a piece of wood. He threw it into the water, and the water became fit to drink" (Exodus 15:25).*

Isn't that a unique solution? Boiling and filtering the water sounds more logical than chucking a piece of wood into it, but God's ways are not like ours. His peculiar solution was intentional and for our benefit.

Every story in the Bible, in some way, points forward to the main story of the Bible - that Jesus would suffer, die, and rise again to save His people from their sins, and to transform us into His image. We, humans, are in a desperate situation because of our sin, but God loved us, so He gave us Jesus who died on the cross, a piece of wood, to save us, rescue us, heal us and deliver us, and in this case, transform our bitterness into sweetness.

Just as God came to the aid of the Israelites, transforming their bitter water into sweet with a piece of wood, so God came to our rescue by sending His beloved Son to die on a piece of wood. But unlike the Israelites who experienced the transformation of bitter waters only once through the wood, Jesus' cross would be the means of life transformation for people from every tribe and nation eternally. The cross is the Solution for the bitterness of your life.

> *"He himself bore our sins in his body **on the tree**, that we might die to sin and live to righteousness. By his wounds you have been healed" (1 Peter 2:24 ESV).*

Application

Are you struggling with feelings of sorrow for a deep betrayal? Are you disillusioned or disheartened by the circumstances of life? Have you been insulted or mistreated and are now replaying the events and reliving the hurt? Come to the cross and behold your Lord, experiencing your betrayal, enduring the agony of defeat for you. He was hurt for you. Now see Him reaching out to you in eternal love, offering to make an exchange with you. Your sorrow, for His joy. The death of your dream, for the resurrection power of the living Christ.

Are you living in bitterness? Trapped by the pain of old and new offenses, and weary of the burden they are to you? Come to the cross of Christ and receive Jesus' sacrificial love and healing into the bitter waters of your heart. Look to Jesus and see that He bore your sorrow and the offense against you on the cross. The debt has been paid.

You can release your offender, even if they are not sorry for what they have done or you think they don't deserve forgiveness. The reason you can forgive your offender is that you aren't extending forgiveness based on the worthiness of your offender, but based upon the worthiness of your Savior. Further, justice has been served at the cross, or God will bring it at the proper time. You can, like Jesus, entrust yourself to the One that judges justly (1 Peter 2:23) and experience the sweetness of freedom that flows from Christ's death and resurrection.

Are you grumbling to God about the bitter waters of your life? Angry about your sin struggles, bitter that you didn't get what you wanted or thought you needed? Come to the cross of Christ and receive God's Solution. Jesus alone can satisfy your thirst. He alone can set you free from sin traps and the defiling bitterness that they bring. Look to Jesus and receive the peace that His wounds speak to you. You have not been denied what you need; you have been blessed beyond measure in Christ. He has clothed you in His robes of righteousness.

Look today to the cross of wood on which Jesus died to experience the transformation of your bitter, sin bound heart into a sweet, Spirit-filled one that is overflowing with His love.

Question: How does remembering Christ's death and resurrection on the cross transform your bitter thoughts into sweet ones?

_____

_____

_____

_____

DAY 12:

Looking to Jesus When Wounded

But he was pierced for our transgressions; he was crushed for our iniquities; upon him was the chastisement that brought us peace, and with his wounds, we are healed.
Isaiah 53:5

From the moment that Adam and Eve ate of the forbidden fruit, we humans have been sinning against God and each other. And all this sinning has brought with it much pain and suffering for everyone. Some have been wounded to death, but most of us are the walking wounded—those whose wounds allow us to keep moving (most of the time) despite the crippling effects of sin on our hearts and minds.

Some teach us to "put on a happy face" and "fake it" until we "make it," but we know that faking is just lying. We will never be healed by pretending that we are.

Others tell us that our healing comes by talking about our wounds in therapy. The idea is that we must revisit, examine, and work through our heart wounds with a professional to be healed from them. And while talking about our sin struggles or the sins that have been committed against us might be necessary for us to receive our healing, we cannot talk our way to healing (Jeremiah 6:14).

Still, others tell us to pursue our healing through hard work. We are instructed to "work the program" and try all manner of self-help approaches, but the problem with this approach is that we eventually wear ourselves out. At the end of all our work, we still feel bad about our sin or the sins committed against us.

But there is a way that is powerful and effective for healing our heart wounds, whether they are self-inflicted or received at the hands of others.

That way is to come to the cross of Jesus Christ and look up! When you look at the cross, you see that Jesus was "wounded for our transgressions," which means that He paid the penalty for sin. And you see that "by His wounds, we are healed," which means that we are received and loved, forgiven, comforted and made whole through Christ's death and resurrection.

Illustration

When Jesus was on this earth, He had an encounter with a woman who had been bleeding for twelve years. "*And a woman was there who had been subject to bleeding for twelve years. She had suffered a great deal under the care of many doctors and had spent all she had, yet instead of getting better she grew worse*" (Mark 5:25-26).

This poor woman was sick and bleeding for many years. She tried to get help for her condition, spending all that she had, all to no avail. But then she heard about Jesus, and notice what she did:

> "*When she heard about Jesus, she came up behind him in the crowd and touched his cloak, because she thought, "If I just touch his clothes, I will be healed." Immediately her bleeding stopped, and she felt in her body that she was freed from her suffering.*" Mark 5:27-29 (NIV)

This woman exercised faith, believing that Jesus was a great Physician who could heal her wounds when no person in her past could. She reached out and touched Jesus' cloak, and immediately she was healed; that is, she was freed from her suffering.

Before she went on her way, Jesus said to her, "*Daughter, your faith has healed you. Go in peace and be freed from your suffering* (Mark 5:34).

Application

Are you suffering today with heart wounds that drain and discourage you? Are you despairing that you can ever experience healing? Have you spent time, energy, and money trying to find healing? Receive this good word today - there is healing for you at the cross of Christ. Look to Jesus now to receive it.

At the cross, you will see that Jesus has taken all the wounds of sin in His own body on the tree. He took on all the abuse you've endured, the self-loathing and feelings of worthlessness, all the anger, rage, and hate. Christ took to Himself all the injuries of body, heart, and mind that you would ever experience. He suffered bodily pain and agony of soul on the cross so that you, dear friend, would be healed. Jesus tasted death itself to heal you; that's how much He loves you. If you want to experience your healing, reach out to Jesus in faith believing that by His wounds you are healed.

Do you have self-inflicted heart wounds? By your own sinful behavior, have you destroyed your life or the lives of others? Have you exhausted yourself trying to find healing only to discover that you are no better and perhaps even worse off than before? There is healing for you, too, at the cross of Christ. At the cross, you will see that Jesus was pierced for your transgressions. He was bruised for your sins. The punishment that brings you peace was poured out on Him. By His wounds, you are healed! Jesus has reversed all your wrongs. He has set things right by His atoning death. He has removed your sins and given you His righteousness. You've only to look to the cross of Christ and believe the better word than the blood of Abel speaks to you. Look to Jesus now and see that love, forgiveness, and healing are yours in Christ.

Question: How does looking to Jesus bring healing to the wounds of your life?

Looking to Jesus When Needing to Forgive

Bear with each other and forgive one another if any of you has a grievance against someone. Forgive as the Lord forgave you. Colossians 3:13

The forgiveness of our sins is a foundational tenet of our Christian faith. We have all sinned. We deserve punishment, but in love, God sent Jesus to die on the cross to pay our sin debt. As believers, we rejoice in our forgiveness! We frequently thank God in our songs and prayers for the forgiveness we receive through Christ and rightly so.

But what happens when we need to extend forgiveness to others? The need arises every day on some level, usually multiple times a day, and frequently for the same offense. Maybe our spouse is unkind, our child is disrespectful, or a friend betrays us. Perhaps forgiveness comes easy for these small offenses. We forgive and move on without too much difficulty.

But at some point, we each face a forgiveness opportunity that seems impossible. Perhaps the offense against us is criminal: someone steals from us, abuses us, assaults us. Or maybe it is deeply personal, our character is attacked in a public and destructive way, or our spouse betrays us. How can we forgive when we are deeply wounded? We find our answer, friend, at the foot of the cross!

When we are hurting, it is easy to forget our own sin that needed forgiveness. In our pain, we forget that Jesus purchased our forgiveness with His own blood. He died so that we could receive forgiveness for our sins. Forgiveness means that someone has to die. Jesus died physically; we die to ourselves.

Illustration

In the book of Genesis, we read about a man named Joseph. Joseph's brothers were very jealous of him and wanted to kill him. *"But they saw him in the distance, and before he reached them, they plotted to kill him. "Here comes that dreamer!" they said to each other. "Come now, let's kill him and throw him into one of these cisterns and say that a ferocious animal devoured him. Then we'll see what comes of his dreams"* (Genesis 37:18-20). The brothers ended up selling Joseph into the hands of foreigners who were slave-traders. He was treated poorly and falsely accused. Then, *"Joseph's master took him and put him in prison, the place where the king's prisoners were confined"* (Genesis 39:20).

While in prison, Joseph helped another prisoner, relaying the interpretation of his dream from God, assuring the prisoner that he would be restored to his place of service to the king. In return, Joseph asked that the prisoner remember him. *"But when all goes well with you, remember me and show me kindness; mention me to Pharaoh and get me out of this prison. I was forcibly carried off from the land of the Hebrews, and even here, I have done nothing to deserve being put in a dungeon"* (Genesis 40:14-15). But *"the chief cupbearer, however, did not remember Joseph; he forgot him"* (Genesis 40:23).

Can you imagine how you might have felt if you were Joseph? Betrayed by family, falsely accused, wrongly imprisoned, forgotten for years. And yet Joseph forgave them all, from his heart.

Notice some of the contrasts between Joseph and his brothers. His brothers pushed Joseph away, but Joseph drew them near (Genesis 45:4). The brothers treated Joseph harshly; he treated them lovingly. They pushed Joseph down into a pit, but he drew them up out of their land of famine into the place of plenty (Genesis 46). They stripped Joseph of his coat, but *"to each of them, he gave new clothing"* (Genesis 45:20). They wanted to kill Joseph, but he saved their lives (Genesis 50:20).

Joseph was eventually exalted to the right hand of Pharaoh. To the end, he was good to his brothers even though they had done evil to him. The reason Joseph could forgive is that he understood God's plan in all events, including the sin of his brothers against him. *"You intended to harm me, but God intended it for good to accomplish what is now being done, the saving of many lives. So then, don't be afraid. I will provide for you and your children." And he reassured them and spoke kindly to them"* (Genesis 50:20-21).

Joseph's life story is given to show you the gospel of Jesus Christ. In Joseph's life, we see one who was loved by his father but hated by his brothers, sold into the hands of Gentiles for pieces of silver, treated badly, falsely accused, unjustly punished, and placed between two criminals. Then he was raised out of the pit and exalted to the right hand of Pharaoh, where he became the lord and savior of all who came to him.

Oh, dear friend, rejoice that Jesus is greater than Joseph. Jesus forgives your every offense, loves and cares for you, and provides for your every need, but also gives you His Spirit, and all this allows you to forgive others, love your enemies, and bless those that curse you.

Application

Are you holding on to an offense today? Have you been nursing a grudge or treating someone according to their sins against you? Jesus invites you into deeper intimacy with Him today.

Look to Jesus and hear Him calling you to fellowship with Him in His sufferings, to become like Him in His death (Philippians 3:10). Look to Jesus and remember how great a sin debt that He has forgiven you. See the blood that He shed. Look into His loving eyes as He willingly sacrifices Himself to save you. See His blood that covers a multitude of sins - yours and your offenders.

Now out of the abundance of love and forgiveness that you have received, follow Christ and die to yourself. Forgive your offender before God as God has forgiven you in Christ Jesus and experience the sweetness of entrusting yourself to the One who judges justly (1 Peter 2:23). Experience the power of Christ's resurrection as you extend forgiveness to those who have sinned against you.

Question: Who is God leading you to forgive as you have been forgiven today?

_____

_____

_____

_____

Looking to Jesus When Feeling Discouraged

Be strong and courageous. Do not be afraid; do not be discouraged, for the Lord your God will be with you wherever you go." Joshua 1:9

*D*iscouragement is something that we all face at some point in our lives. We try something, fail, and get discouraged. Others fail us; we get discouraged. Unexpected illnesses, natural disasters, financial mishaps, global crises can all lead us to discouragement.

In response to discouragement, some people fall into despair. They collapse under the weight of shame. They allow their grief to crush their spirit or resign themselves to their dismal fate. They give up. For the believer, this is the trap of unbelief.

Others answer discouragement by doubling down and working harder. They look for solutions. "I can fix it!" is their cry. They rally under pressure; they consume self-help books and seek out guidance on how they can improve themselves or their situation. And while self-sufficiency seems laudable from a distance, those who believe in Christ know that it, too, is a snare.

The biblical answer to discouragement, dear friend, is found in the death and resurrection of Jesus Christ.

Paul wrote to the church at Corinth, "We are afflicted in every way, but not crushed; perplexed, but not driven to despair; persecuted, but not forsaken; struck down, but not destroyed..." (2 Corinthians 4:8-9). He then goes on to explain the reason for their resilience and hope, "always carrying in the body the death of Jesus, so that the life of Jesus may also be manifested in our bodies. For we who live are always being given over to death for Jesus' sake, so that the life of Jesus also may be manifested in our mortal flesh." (2 Corinthians 4:10-11).

Do you see it? As believers, we carry around the death of Christ in our hearts so that His life will be manifested in us. We remember His death on the cross to give us eternal life, and this gives us hope that He will sustain us in our temporary life. We understand that the worst moment in history—the crucifixion of the Son of God—is the most significant, loving, life-saving moment of all time, and this gives us hope that our worst moment (whatever it is) will also be made beautiful in God's time. Jesus endured the cross but rose again three days later. As believers, we believe in this resurrection not only for Christ, not only for our future but also for today amid our current circumstances.

Illustration

Mary and Martha were friends of Jesus, and in John 11, we learn the circumstances surrounding the death of their brother Lazarus. Jesus came to the funeral, and Mary did not come out to see Him. Martha said to Jesus, *"if you had been here, my brother would not have died"* (John 11:21). Both sisters were no doubt upset with Jesus and discouraged, believing Jesus could have healed Lazarus had He only come sooner.

Jesus told Martha that her brother would rise again, and Martha replied with the typical Jewish understanding of a resurrection at the end of time: *"I know he will rise again in the resurrection at the last day"* (John 11:24).

Jesus told Martha, and tells us today, that He, Himself, is the resurrection, and that resurrection power is available today, right now, for everyone who believes. *"Jesus said to her, 'I am the resurrection and the life. The one who believes in me will live, even though they die; and whoever lives by believing in me will never die'"* (John 11:25-26).

Friend, Jesus not only died to make you right with God but He has also risen from the dead and is now alive forever. Resurrection power is for you, right now, today! A believer is never hopeless for we walk with One who is the resurrection and the life, One who ever lives to intercede for us, and because

He lives we can face tomorrow! Look to Jesus, and find in Him your living hope! *"In his great mercy, he has given us new birth into a living hope through the resurrection of Jesus Christ from the dead"* (1 Peter 1:3).

Application

Are you discouraged? Confounded by your circumstances? Are you facing difficulties that are beyond you? Are you tempted just to give up and abandon yourself to despair? Look to Jesus and see that He died to rescue You from discouragement and despair; He has not brought you to this place to forsake you. He loves you. He has brought you into the place of need because He is going to provide for you.

Do not listen to the lies of the evil one; you are not alone. You are loved! Jesus knows your situation, and He is sympathetic. Look to Him, remember His death on the cross and His resurrection, carry this truth close to your heart and in the front of your mind so that you will have hope and not despair. Believe in Jesus and HIs goodness. Trust Him; He is worthy. As you carry the death of Jesus in your mind, you will see the life of Jesus revealed in you.

Are you working yourself to death trying to save yourself only to find yourself losing ground? Are you weary of trying to fix things, control everything and everyone? Is discouragement overtaking you? Look to Jesus and find rest for your weariness.

Jesus cried out from the cross in a loud voice, "It is finished!" Through His death on the cross, He completed His rescue mission. He lived the perfect life we could not live and died the death we deserved so that we would be reconciled to God and have eternal encouragement in Him. In Christ, we are righteous. Now we must strive to enter His rest (Hebrews 4:11).

Do not press for self-reliance, friend, but instead, strive for dependence on Christ. As you abide in Jesus, you will bear the fruits of repentance and the fruits of the Spirit you desire. As you rest in Christ's finished work on the cross, you will find great encouragement for your heart, because you are trusting that God's purpose will be done on earth as it is in heaven.

"Therefore, brothers, since we have confidence to enter the holy places by the blood of Jesus, by the new and living way that he

opened for us through the curtain, that is, through his flesh, and since we have a great priest over the house of God, let us draw near with a true heart in full assurance of faith, with our hearts sprinkled clean from an evil conscience and our bodies washed with pure water. Let us hold fast the confession of our hope without wavering, for he who promised is faithful." Hebrews 10:19-23

Question: How are you encouraged when you look to Jesus and His finished work on the cross?

_____

_____

_____

_____

Looking to Jesus When Feeling Discontent

"For the sake of Christ, then, I am content with weaknesses, insults, hardships, persecutions, and calamities. For when I am weak, then I am strong." 2 Corinthians 12:10

*T*he world values beauty and strength. Advertisers frequently appeal to our vanity by marketing their products as that which will restore our youth and vitality. So when we are weak (emotionally, physically, or spiritually), our natural inclination is to feel shame and to want to escape it.

Our culture also abhors insults, hardships, persecution, and calamities. These are things to be avoided, not accepted. Our society encourages us to stand up for our rights! The world tells us that if we work together, we can overcome disease, hate, global terrorism, and even natural disasters.

And yet, history has proven that despite all man's efforts toward peace, equality, and prosperity, abuse remains. We are expressing the same complaints of our forefathers. We cannot escape our mortality, suffering, injustice, and pain through anything this world has to offer. This can leave us feeling discontent in many areas of our lives.

And yet, Paul wrote to the church at Philippi, *"...I have learned in whatever situation I am to be content. I know how to be brought low, and I know how to abound. In any and every circumstance, I have learned the secret of facing plenty and hunger, abundance, and need." Philippians 4:11-12*

So, what is this secret? Where can we look to find contentment amid the clamoring and chaos of our world?

The secret of facing every situation in contentment is Jesus Christ. When we fully embrace the truth that we died with Christ on the cross and rose again to a new life in Him, we no longer desire to escape our weaknesses, difficulties, persecutions, and pain because we see things differently.

Hebrews 2:8-10 explains, *"Now in putting everything in subjection to him, he left nothing outside his control. At present, we do not yet see everything in subjection to him.* **But we see him** *who for a little while was made lower than the angels, namely Jesus, crowned with glory and honor because of the suffering of death so that by the grace of God he might taste death for everyone. For it was fitting that he, for whom and by whom all things exist, in bringing many sons to glory, should make the founder of their salvation perfect through suffering."*

Jesus suffered and died on the cross to bring us to glory. *"If we live, we live for the LORD; and if we die, we die for the LORD. So, whether we live or die, we belong to the LORD."* (Romans 14:8) Jesus is the object of our love and our life. When we look and see Him loving us unto death on the cross, we know that we are loved and forgiven, and this fills us with a contentment that is constant regardless of our circumstances.

Friend, you died with Christ and rose in Him to a new life. A life where tragedy becomes a triumph, obstacles become opportunities, and trouble becomes a testimony to God's mercy, love, grace, and faithfulness.

Illustration

In the book of Daniel, we read the account of three Hebrew young men who were taken captive to Babylon, had their names changed to Shadrack, Meshack, and Abednego, and were commanded to bow down and worship a golden statue of Nebuchadnezzar. Their resistance meant facing the wrath of the king and being thrown into a furnace of fire.

They refused to bow to the statue, saying, *"If we are thrown into the blazing furnace, the God we serve is able to deliver us from it, and he will deliver us from Your Majesty's hand. But even if he does not, we want you to know, Your Majesty, that we will not serve your gods or worship the image of gold you have set up"* (Daniel 3:17-18).

They refused to serve the gods of the Babylonians nor bow down to the statue of gold, and so they were bound and thrown into the fire. The fire was so hot it killed the soldiers who threw the three Hebrew men into the fire.

God performed a miracle to keep the three Hebrew men from being burned, and they walked out of the furnace, having lost only that which bound them. They were freed in the fire, and free when they came out.

But the most significant point of the story is what the King, who had thrown the men into the fire, saw when he looked into the furnace:

"Then King Nebuchadnezzar leaped to his feet in amazement and asked his advisers, 'Weren't there three men that we tied up and threw into the fire?'

They replied, 'Certainly, Your Majesty.'

He said, 'Look! I see four men walking around in the fire, unbound and unharmed, and the fourth looks like a son of the gods'" (Daniel 3:24-25).

The Son of God, Jesus Christ Himself, had gone into the fire to rescue these three Hebrews and brought them out safely.

The Hebrew men had their minds, hearts, and eyes set on God before they went into the fire, so they were content to face death; they did not resist the persecution. And in the fire, they saw Jesus, the Son of God, face to face. Jesus saved them and set them free.

About six hundred years later, the Son of God went into another fire, the fire of God's wrath against sin. He went to a criminal's cross and was baptized by fire as He endured not only the beatings of the Romans and the mockings of the Jewish leaders but also the intense hatred of a holy God against our sin. This time, the fire of God's wrath completely consumed Jesus, and in so doing, it set us free. All who believe are free from sin's penalty, free from guilt, and are being freed from sin's power. We come to the cross, watch the fire consuming the Son of God, and we are content to face the temporary hardships and calamities of this life because we know that not one spark of that eternal fire of wrath will reach us; indeed, nothing of that fire even touches us.

> *"...the fire had not harmed their bodies, nor was a hair of their heads singed; their robes were not scorched, and there was no smell of fire on them"* (Daniel 3:27).

Just as Jesus entered the fire to rescue the three Hebrew young men, so He has entered the fire of God's wrath to rescue you from it. He died in it and, at the same time, freed you from it. Now, find your contentment in Jesus and His finished work.

Application

Have you been seeking relief from the difficulties of life in earthly things? Are you comfort eating, drinking to forget, seeking satisfaction in sexual impurity? Are you living a life of self-loathing, bound up with bitterness about what others have done to you, seething in anger, coveting others' circumstances, or living in hate or resentment?

Look to Jesus, dear friend. Look to His cross and see Jesus pouring out His life to set your free. See that you are safe in His love, accepted in His righteousness, and free in His forgiveness.

Come to the cross of Jesus and see Him facing all the hardships of life and living through them perfectly and attributing that perfection to you. See Jesus enduring all the persecutions, unjust mockings, and beatings, taking on all your weaknesses and failings and dying with them. Now see Him rising with healing in His wings for you. Learn contentment from your Beloved! Embrace the new life that Jesus has purchased for you. Rejoice in your King Jesus, who never leaves you nor forsakes you.

When you experience trials, hardships, or persecution, you can be fully content, for Jesus is in the trial with you. Jesus brings freedom to you in your difficulties. He is in control; He will sustain you and bring you through safely. You are loved!

"Keep your life free from love of money and be content with what you have, for he has said, "I will never leave you nor forsake you." So we can confidently say, "The Lord is my helper; I will not fear; what can man do to me?" Hebrews 13: 5-6

Question: How does focusing on Christ and His cross foster contentment in your heart today?

_____

_____

_____

_____

Looking to Jesus When Feeling Rejected

*"He was despised and rejected by men, a man of sorrows
and acquainted with grief; and as one from whom men
hide their faces he was despised, and we esteemed him
not." Isaiah 53:3*

Rejection is a universal experience that comes in many different ways. We might experience emotional or physical rejection from a parent, spouse, friend, or child. Or perhaps we don't get accepted to the school, the group, or the place of employment that we want. Or maybe our love is spurned or goes unrequited. We can be rejected based on our faith, our beliefs, our appearance, and even for reasons that have nothing to do with us.

Suicide, school shootings, and violence in the wake of broken relationships are evidence of the deep emotions that rejection elicits. Even the threat of rejection is enough to provoke anger and aggression in some.

Some of us experience more rejection than others, but we all face it on some level, and it hurts. Rejection can wound us and create painful memories, which can affect the way we see ourselves and our circumstances and can create barriers in our relationships with others, including God.

The good news is that there is hope for those who look to Jesus and put their faith in Him. Jesus died on the cross to bring healing to our hearts for our own rejection of God in preference for sin, as well as to heal the wounds that a lifetime of rejections left on our hearts.

Jesus came into our world and experienced every rejection possible. He knows our pain intimately and so He can address it like no one else can. Look to the cross of Christ and see.

Jesus was despised by His own, rejected by those He came to save. As He hung on the cross, all our sins, sorrows, and griefs were laid on Him so much so that He was no longer recognizable as a human (Isaiah 52:14). He became utterly disfigured by our sin, and at that moment, by eternal agreement, God the Father rejected and forsook His own beloved Son so that you, dear friend, would be received and accepted for all time.

Illustration

In Matthew 26 and John 12, we can read the account of Mary of Bethany, the sister of Martha and Lazarus, who understood the message of the cross, that she, though sinful, was forgiven, loved, and accepted by God, through the upcoming death of Jesus. So she took a bottle of costly ointment and broke it, pouring out the contents on Jesus in preparation for His burial. But not everyone appreciated Mary or her sacrifice.

> *"When the disciples saw this, they were indignant. 'Why this waste?' they asked. 'This perfume could have been sold at a high price and the money given to the poor'" (Matthew 26:8-9 NIV).*

These disciples didn't yet understand Jesus' mission, so they rejected Mary and scorned her offering and expression of love for Jesus. But Jesus, who was rejected repeatedly by man and who was facing the cross and rejection by God, rushed to Mary's defense:

> *Aware of this, Jesus said to them, "Why are you bothering this woman? She has done a beautiful thing to me. The poor you will always have with you, but you will not always have me. When she poured this perfume on my body, she did it to prepare me for burial. Truly I tell you, wherever this gospel is preached throughout the world, what she has done will also be told, in memory of her" (Matthew 26:10-13 NIV).*

Like Mary, we will face rejection in this life, but we can look to Jesus when rejected, and be confident that He will be with us through it all. He sees us, He remembers us, and He comes to our defense when we are rejected.

Application

Have you been rejected? Is your heart hurting because of it? Jesus sees, He knows, and He cares. He was rejected for you and now lives to defend you. He came to bind up the brokenhearted and receive the rejected.

Remind yourself that you are chosen by God and dearly loved (Colossians 3:12)! In love, God sent Jesus to this world to die in your place to set you free from sin, to clothe you in righteousness, to restore your relationship with God. He has removed the curse of rejection from you and replaced it with full acceptance (Galatians 3:13, Romans 14:3, Ephesians 1:5-7).

You are loved with an everlasting love, and no one can separate you from it (Romans 8:38-39), and out of the abundance of love and acceptance that you have in Jesus, you can seek to overcome evil with good (Romans 12:21).

Are you suffering from a recent rejection or a painful one in your past? Come to Jesus and fellowship with Him in His sufferings. Your pain and rejection give you unique insight into the sufferings that Jesus endured to set you free. Embrace your Savior and allow your pain to push you into a deeper relationship with Him (Philippians 3:10).

Has your spouse or friend betrayed you? Are your adult children ignoring your counsel and treating you with disdain? Are your co-workers excluding you or talking about you in an unkind way? Are people in your community or church hurting you by their actions or words? Look to Jesus and follow His lead.

> "For to this, you have been called, because Christ also suffered for you, leaving you an example, so that you might follow in his steps. He committed no sin; neither was deceit found in his mouth. When he was reviled, he did not revile in return; when he suffered, he did not threaten but continued entrusting himself to him who judges justly. He himself bore our sins in his body on the tree that we might die to sin and live to righteousness. By his wounds, you have been healed." 1 Peter 2:21-24

Go out of your way to bless those who reject you (Romans 12:14). Do good to them. Pray for them (Matthew 5:44). You don't know, but what your sacrifice of love and kindness might be what God uses to draw your offender out of the darkness and into the light of His love (1 Corinthians 7:16).

Remember, too, that God ordained the rejection of Jesus for a marvelous purpose - the saving and sanctification and transformation of many lives. Our sufferings have a higher purpose also, and God has provided Christ and His cross as the means by which we can endure and not grow weary in doing what is right (Hebrews 12:3).

> *Jesus said to them, "Have you never read in the Scriptures: "'The stone that the builders rejected has become the cornerstone; this was the Lord's doing, and it is marvelous in our eyes'? Matthew 21:42*

Question: How does looking to the cross of Christ enable you to show love and kindness to those who have rejected and hurt you?

Looking to Jesus When Feeling Anxious

*"Anxiety in a man's heart weighs him down, but a good
word makes him glad." Proverbs 12:25*

S ome people teach that Christians are exempt from the worries of this world, but it just isn't true. We live in a fallen world that is full of trouble (John 16:33). Disease, heartache, financial loss, and all manner of sin touch our lives daily and produce the same anxieties that unbelievers experience.

These anxieties trouble each of us in different ways and to different degrees. Some of us encounter anxiety so intense that it manifests in physical symptoms such as pain, hives, profuse sweating, or the inability to eat, sleep, or even breathe well. But we all share the common root of our anxieties, which is fear. We fear pain, loss, the unknown, etc. and these fears produce anxiety in our hearts, minds, and bodies.

But even though we face the same anxieties as unbelievers, there is a real distinctive for us who believe in Jesus - the gospel! The death and resurrection of Jesus to secure our eternal well-being are the "good word" that makes our hearts glad and relieves our anxieties if we learn to focus there. *Anxiety in a man's heart weighs him down, but a good word makes him glad." Proverbs 12:25*

Paul wrote to the young evangelist Timothy, who was prone to anxiety, "... *for God gave us a spirit not of fear but of power and love and self-control. Therefore do not be ashamed of the testimony about our Lord, nor of me his prisoner, but share in suffering for the gospel by the power of God, who saved us and called us to a holy calling, not because of our works but because of his own purpose and grace, which he gave us in Christ Jesus before the ages began, and which now has been manifested through the appearing of our Savior Christ Jesus, who abolished death and brought life and immortality to light through the gospel," 2 Timothy 1:7-10*

Notice how the Scriptures connect the death and resurrection of Jesus to our freedom from fear and anxiety. Death, our worst and final enemy, has been abolished by Jesus on the cross so we can trust that He has also dealt with all the other things that cause anxiety in us.

Through His death on the cross, Jesus gave us His Spirit, and Jesus' Spirit produces in us supernatural strength, love, and self-control. We don't work harder to overcome our anxiety; we focus on and rest in the finished work of our Jesus.

Friend, though they do not feel that way, your anxieties are common, and they are not your problem. Your problem comes when you hang on to your concerns and focus on them. To be free of your anxieties, you must see Jesus high and lifted up, dying on the cross to bring you peace, shedding His blood to atone for your sin and set you free. See Him rising from the dead victorious, having conquered all things in life that cause anxiety. When you fix your thoughts on Jesus, He will overwhelm your anxieties with His love.

If you want to combat your anxieties and win, you must look to Jesus on the cross, and believe that God is for you. Look now and see the perfect love of Jesus displayed on the cross and allow His sacrificial love to cast out all your fear (1 John 4:13-19). If you are in Christ, friend, the victory is yours. Sin and death are defeated. Your situation, no matter how distressing, is temporary, but God's love for you is eternal.

Illustration

In the book of Joshua, we read about an alliance of five kings who were summoned to help the King of Jerusalem fight against the Gibeonites. The Gibeonites were very anxious and alarmed to see such a strong alliance of king-nations gathering together against them, and so they sent word to Joshua, the leader of Israel, saying the following:

> *"Do not abandon your servants. Come up to us quickly and save us! Help us, because all the Amorite kings from the hill country have joined forces against us" (Joshua 10:6).*

Day 17: Looking to Jesus When Feeling Anxious

The Lord was with Joshua and fought for him, so the battle was won: "*The Lord threw them into confusion before Israel, so Joshua and the Israelites defeated them completely at Gibeon*" (Joshua 10:10).

Now notice what Joshua did with the five captured kings. He instructed his chief fighters:

> "*'Come near; put your feet on the necks of these kings.' Then they came near and put their feet on their necks. And Joshua said to them, 'Do not be afraid or dismayed; be strong and courageous. For thus, the Lord will do to all your enemies against whom you fight.' And afterward Joshua struck them and put them to death, and he hanged them on five trees. And they hung on the trees until evening.*"

These five kings were hung on trees, and God's Word had decreed that anyone hung on a tree must not be left on it overnight, for whoever is hung on a tree is under God's curse (Deuteronomy 21:22-23).

The hanging of the five men on the trees was God's assurance to the soldiers that He was for them, that He would fight their battles, that they would be victorious over all enemies whom they fought. The impression of those men hanging on the trees no doubt stayed with them, giving them the courage that they would be triumphant in their battles.

Like the Gibeonites, we, too, have many things that can cause us to be anxious and fearful. But we turn to the Lord and call upon His Name. Jesus is our Joshua; He bids us come and put our foot on the neck of that which caused us anxiety, and He assures us that it is defeated. Then He shows us a King hanging on a tree. Jesus is our King hanging on the cross, under the curse of God (Galatians 3:13). His death on the cross is the assurance that God is for us, that He will defeat every enemy, that we will be more than conquerors in life because Jesus loved us unto death. Let the impression of Jesus on the cross, and Jesus risen from the dead, stay with you, focus on it, and as you do, it will give you courage in the face of fear. We are "*more than conquerors through him who loved us*" (Romans 8:37).

Application

Are you anxious about many things today? Is your anxiety causing you pain (mental, emotional, or physical)? Do your anxieties keep you from enjoying life or prevent you from building the kingdom of God? Look to Jesus! See that on the cross, Jesus has defeated your enemies. These things that cause you anxiety might be real or only possibilities, but either way, Jesus has conquered them. Look to the empty tomb and see that Jesus has risen victorious, and you were raised with Him (Colossians 3:1). God has given you His Spirit to strengthen and comfort you in times of distress. He will hold you together and keep you safe in His love (Colossians 1:17, Romans 8:35-39).

Are you feeling buried beneath a weight of anxiety and care? Does it seem that the troubles in your life are suffocating you and hindering your relationship with God and others? Look to Jesus! See His nail-pierced hands reaching out for you, lifting you up and out of your pit of worry. Hear Him inviting you to draw near to Him. Feel Him breathing out His last breath to give you a life filled with His peace. Bring your cares to Him, to entrust yourself, and those you love to Him. He is faithful (2 Thessalonians 3:3). Jesus can keep you (Jude 1:24).

Is the devil filling your mind with troubling thought? Would you have a calm and quiet heart and mind? Cast your anxieties at the foot of Jesus' cross and receive from Jesus heart-filling, mind-calming, peace-giving, joy-producing love, and freedom. Pour out your troubles and open your heart and mind to the redeeming love of Jesus that does not abandon you in trouble, but protects and surrounds you with songs of deliverance (Psalm 32:7).

There is freedom from anxiety in Christ, dear friend, but you will not experience it unless you come to the cross of Jesus, release your fears, and receive the peace that Jesus purchased for you.

Do not be anxious about anything, but in every situation, by prayer and petition, with thanksgiving, present your requests to God. And the peace of God, which transcends all understanding, will guard your hearts and your minds in Christ Jesus. Philippians 4:6-7 NIV

Question: List out the anxieties that are troubling you today. How does looking to Jesus alleviate your fears and calm your mind?

_____

_____

_____

_____

DAY 18:

Looking to Jesus When Stumbling

"For we all stumble in many ways." James 3:2a
"...the righteous falls seven times and rises again" Proverbs 24:16a

$\mathcal{E}$very week it seems we hear stories of pastors, teachers, and leaders stepping down or removed from their posts due to moral failures of some kind. And while we might be tempted to shake our heads and exclaim our disappointment, if we are honest, we know that we too are prone to stumbles and falls.

The world, the devil, and our own flesh all conspire together to wear us down, distract us, trip us up, and trap us. We get weary, become downcast, lose sight of Jesus, and then stumble along the way. We get distracted by temporary things such as work, worries, and desires, take our eyes off Jesus, and down we go. It happens faster than we think possible and far more often than we want to admit.

Some of us wallow when we fall. We give in to despair and foolishly reason that since we have fallen, we might as well give up on walking altogether. What started as a fall turns into a foray into enemy territory where we risk captivity and do damage to ourselves and those around us.

Others of us minimize or deny our falls. We pretend that all is well with us. We go through all the motions of our faith, hoping that no one catches us out. We prop ourselves up with good works and appropriate appearances for as long as possible. We falsely believe that if we just try hard enough, we will get back on our feet, but we quickly discover that we are unable.

But the prophet Micah gives us the right response to a fall, *"But as for me, I will look to the Lord; I will wait for the God of my salvation; my God will hear me.*

Rejoice not over me, O my enemy; when I fall, I shall rise; when I sit in darkness, the Lord will be a light to me. I will bear the indignation of the Lord because I have sinned against him until he pleads my cause and executes judgment for me. He will bring me out to the light; I shall look upon his vindication." Micah 7:7-9

In Micah 7:7-8, Jesus is speaking through His prophet, Micah, anticipating His death on the cross. On the cross, it was as if He "fell," though He was the only one who never did. At the cross, Jesus "fell" under the weight of our sin. He hung in darkness for three hours under the judgment of God while bearing the indignation of God's wrath over our sin. Then He rose again on the third day and was brought out into the light, having been vindicated by God, His Father.

When Micah himself fell, he said, *"I will look to the Lord"* and *"I shall look upon His vindication,"* and so, like Jesus, Micah would *"rise again"* and be brought out into the light.

Friend, falls are unavoidable, and we end up in darkness by our sin. But by looking to Jesus on the cross, we see both *His condemnation* and *our justification*. We see Jesus risen from the dead and *"pleading our cause"* before the Father, and so we rise again, knowing there is no condemnation for us.

When you fall, look to Jesus and see that on the cross, He paid your sin debt and bore the indignation of the Lord for you. Indeed, Jesus has taken all the wrath of the Father so that there is none left for you. There is no condemnation for you because Jesus stood in your place, and judgment was executed on Him. In Heaven, Jesus presents His wounds and pleads your cause. You are justified from all falls and fully vindicated by the work of Jesus! He has raised and will continue to raise you to walk by His Spirit.

Illustration

There are many illustrations of people falling in sin throughout the Scriptures because every human except Jesus has fallen at some point. For example, Moses was zealous for God and His people, but then he murdered an Egyptian and ran away to hide for 40 years. But at the right time, the Lord appeared to Moses in a burning bush and restored Moses to a place of usefulness. David, the man after God's own heart, fell to adultery and murder, yet looked to the Lord and was restored.

Peter boasted that he would never fall away from Jesus, but just a few hours later, he fell to denying Christ repeatedly (Matthew 26:30-75). Three times Peter swore that he did not know Jesus. But then Jesus came, and Peter was restored by grace and told to feed Jesus' lambs, made useful in ministry despite and even through his fall.

We could continue listing the many people who fell in sin and experienced the consequences and suffering that a fall into sin brings, but what is essential to see is that each one, without exception, was found by Jesus and restored by God's grace and love. You will be, too.

> *"And the God of all grace, who called you to his eternal glory in Christ, after you have suffered a little while, will himself restore you and make you strong, firm and steadfast. To him be the power for ever and ever. Amen." 1 Peter 5:10*

Application

Do you find yourself fallen by the way, tripped or trapped by some sin that hinders you? Look to Jesus and see His heart of love pierced for you. See Jesus dying to pay for the sin in which you stumbled. See Him liberating you from the penalty of your sin. See yourself dying with Him and rising with Him. Remember that you are dead to sin; it is not your master. Let the grace of Jesus flow to you and teach you to say no to ungodliness and worldly lusts. See the love of Jesus on the cross and let it lift you out of your pit to walk again in the Light.

Are you weary and stumbling in your walk? Are you tired of the pressures of this life, distracted by the cares of the world? Look to Jesus and experience His sacrificial love flowing to you from the cross. See the blood Jesus shed, filling you with faith and hope for a blessed future. See Jesus working for you and in you. See Jesus breathing out His last to breathe life abundant into you. Fix your eyes and your thoughts on Jesus and remember His sacrifice for you, and as you do, His resurrection power will move you and use you to the glory of God

> *"Do you not know? Have you not heard? The Lord is the everlasting God, the Creator of the ends of the earth. He will not grow tired or weary, and his understanding no one can fathom. He gives*

strength to the weary and increases the power of the weak. Even youths grow tired and weary, and young men stumble and fall, but those who hope in the Lord will renew their strength. They will soar on wings like eagles; they will run and not grow weary, they will walk and not be faint." Isaiah 40:28-31

How does looking to Jesus, crucified and risen for you, lift you up today?

_____

_____

_____

_____

Looking to Jesus When Fallen from Grace

*"You who are trying to be justified by the law have been
alienated from Christ; you have fallen away from grace."*
Galatians 5:4

The phrase "fallen from grace" has been dramatically abused throughout time. It is typically used to describe someone who has been scandalized by failure. Politicians caught in lies, athletes cheating, pastors falling, performers faking, etc. but in the context of the Bible to "fall from grace" means to turn from Christ to the law to be made right with God and others.

Have you ever sinned, asked God for forgiveness, but then gone on to work hard to "make it up" to God? This is a fall from grace.

Or maybe you have looked to the death and resurrection of Jesus for salvation, but now you think you need to get a handle on your sin issues by working a program or doing extra good works to balance out your sins. If so, you have fallen from grace.

Have you been offended by the scandalous sin of another, heard of or seen the sinner repent, but resented the forgiveness and restoration they received? Does your personal pain eclipse your ability to rejoice with the sinner that repents? You have fallen from grace.

To "fall from grace" means to turn from Christ and turn to the Law for justification, turning to a pharisaical way of life centered in appearances, the flesh, merit, and self. To "fall from grace" means you are not experiencing the grace that abounds at the cross of Christ, and if you're not experiencing it, you're unable to give it to others.

This was the experience of the believers in Galatia. They started out by "seeing" the picture of Jesus Christ and Him crucified, that Paul had "painted" with gospel words (Galatians 3:1). They believed this message. They were saved by grace alone through faith in Christ crucified, but then they were lured away from the cross with the idea that the law was their guide to perfection. So, Paul writes: *"O foolish Galatians! Who has bewitched you? It was before your eyes that Jesus Christ was publicly portrayed as crucified. Let me ask you this: Did you receive the Spirit by works of the law or by hearing with faith? Are you so foolish? Having begun by the Spirit, are you now being perfected by the flesh?"* Galatians 3:1

Friend, when you lose sight of the cross of Christ, you fall from grace. You do not grow out of the gospel or mature apart from the cross of Christ. You only grow in grace by remaining in the love of Jesus that flows from His cross. *"The only thing that counts is faith expressing itself through love." (Galatians 5:6 NIV)* And *"This is how we know what love is: Jesus Christ laid down his life for us. And we ought to lay down our lives for our brothers and sisters." 1 John 3:16 NIV*

As a believer, you belong to the Lord (Romans 14:8). If you would please God, you must believe in Jesus (John 6:29), experience His love (1 John 4:16), and be compelled by His love (2 Corinthians 5:14). In Christ, grace abounds, and love wins.

The law leads you to condemnation, judgment, and suffering, but on the cross, Christ stood in your place. Jesus fulfilled the law for you and attributed His righteousness to you. Grace abounded to you at the cross; do not be diverted from it now. *"Christ is the end of the Law for righteousness"* (Romans 10:4).

Illustration

In Matthew 18:21-25, Jesus tells the story of a king's servant who owed a great debt to the king. This debt was so substantial the servant could not pay it off, so the king *"took pity on him,"* that is, the king had mercy on him and gave the servant grace. The king forgave this servant his massive debt and put his servant under grace. The servant was forgiven and freed from his financial obligation to the king.

However, the forgiven servant did not embrace the grace shown to him, for he left the king's presence, went out to his fellow servant who owed him a small debt, and demanded immediate payment. When the servant with the little debt could not pay, he was thrown into prison by the first servant.

Perhaps the first servant doubted the reality of the king's grace and thought he should be prepared to pay off his forgiven debt just in case the king changed his mind. Or perhaps he was trying to prove that he was worthy of the grace the king had shown him. Either way, the first servant thought he needed to do more. This is what it means to fall from grace. The evidence that he fell from grace was in how he treated others.

To fall from grace is to refuse to accept or to forget that your sin debt has been paid off by Jesus on the cross, and to seek to do more or earn the grace of God. When we place ourselves under the law, we become harsh and unmerciful like the law. But when we fix our eyes on Jesus, believe and receive His grace, remember He has paid our sin debt in full, we can live in generosity and love with others.

Application

Are you focused on yourself and what you are doing for God? Are you a conviction junkie, always wanting to know what you need to do to please God, but never looking to Christ's finished work, which made you pleasing to Him? Do you resist grace, always wanting to pay your own way, and earn everything you get? Repent of your pride and return to the foot of the cross to remember the supernatural love with which you have been loved. See the nail-pierced hands, feet, and side of Jesus pouring the blood that atoned for your sins. Receive the payment of your sin debt and embrace your freedom in Jesus. Stop working for the love and acceptance of Jesus and start living in the love and acceptance He purchased for you. Grace abounds to you today, dear friend. Receive it and be raised to walk in God's love!

Do you judge others harshly? Are you unable to rejoice in the mercy of God towards sinners? Do you look down on others for their past or current sins or struggles? Look to Jesus and His cross and remember that Jesus paid for your sin with His precious blood. Everything you have, righteousness included, was given to you by grace through the death and resurrection of Jesus. Humble yourself in the love of Jesus and embrace His grace that loves others and wants them to know and experience all the joy and love of belonging to the body of Christ. Don't fall from grace, fall into grace, dear friend.

"For you were called to freedom, brothers. Only do not use your freedom as an opportunity for the flesh, but through love serve one another. For the whole law is fulfilled in one word: "You shall love your neighbor as yourself." Galatians 5:13-14

"Yet I hold this against you: You have forsaken the love you had at first. Consider how far you have fallen! Repent and do the things you did at first." Revelation 2:4-5 NIV

How does looking to Jesus keep you from falling from grace today?

_____

_____

_____

_____

Looking to Jesus When Angry

"But now you must put them all away: anger, wrath, malice, slander, and obscene talk from your mouth." Colossians 3:8

*T*he inciting factors vary, but we are all familiar with sinful anger. Countries wage all manners of war - civil wars, cold wars, trade wars, cyber wars, etc. - led by angry people hungry for more power, money, or resources. Political parties bash each other in anger without shame. Employees go "postal" over perceived injustices in the workplace and lash out in anger. Road rage over drivers who are too slow, too fast, reckless, or just rude is rampant. Children throw tantrums, siblings fight, parents lose it, friends betray.

Sinful anger is frequently found in the body of Christ as well, with quarrels over doctrine and scripture interpretation abounding. Even anger at God is not uncommon, as in the case with Jonah, who was furious with God because of the mercy God showed to the Ninevites who were Israel's enemies.

Indeed, it is surprising if we can make it through a day without encountering sinful anger in some measure. It is easy to recognize. Sinful anger is rooted in the flesh. It protects and serves self. It surfaces in the face of inconvenience, embarrassment, and wounded pride. Sinful anger is punitive and demeaning. It seeks revenge; it is impatient, self-righteous, and demanding. It is ugly, argumentative, sometimes loud, and always destructive.

"Know this, my beloved brothers: let every person be quick to hear, slow to speak, slow to anger; for the anger of man does not produce the righteousness of God." James 1:19-20

The Bible makes it clear that sinful anger is not productive; it does not produce righteousness in our lives or the lives of others. But what can we do when our anger builds to the point of eruption? Is there a way to *"be angry"* about sin and its offense but not sin in response?

The world offers solutions such as venting your anger through exercise or by hitting a pillow or punching bag. They offer tips on breathing out your anger or counting to calm down. They make suggestions for identifying the things that make you angry (wrongly labeling them "triggers") and making a plan to avoid them and manage your anger. And while these recommendations might have the appearance of wisdom and might modify your behavior for a time, they ultimately lack the power to change your heart.

But through the cross of Christ, God has made a way for us to *"Be angry and do not sin."* (Ephesians 4:26a). When we suffer offense of any kind, and we feel anger rising within, we can look to Jesus and His cross to see that God has avenged us through the cross. Look to the cross of Christ and see the ugliness of sin and the wrath of God poured out on Jesus. As you behold the terrible cross of Christ, understand that no anger of yours will ever produce the righteousness that comes through the cross of Christ. Agree with God that His anger is enough and allow His peace to overwhelm and quiet your heart and mind.

Illustration

In 2 Kings 6, we read the account of the war between the country of Aram and God's people, Israel. The King of Aram discovered that Elisha, the prophet, was listening to God, and aiding the people of God to win the war over the king of Aram, so the king of Aram sent an entire army to capture Elisha. The Lord blinded the Arameans and led them to Samaria, totally lost, blind, and confused.

When the king of Israel saw his enemies blind and confused, he asked Elisha, "Shall I kill them, my father? Shall I kill them?" (2 Kings 6:21). You can almost feel his blood lust and his anger against these people who brought war to his door. He wanted to vent his anger and take their lives! Jesus talked about this kind of hate as "heart murder" (Matthew 5:21-30), teaching that if we hate someone, we have murdered them in our hearts.

So what did Elisha say? Would he agree with the Israelite king's desire to kill these men from Aram?

2 Kings 6:22 (NIV) Do not kill them," he answered. "Would you kill those you have captured with your own sword or bow? Set food and water before them so that they may eat and drink and then go back to their master."

Wait! What? Don't kill them, give them a feast? You want me to do good to those who wage war against us? Show love to those who hate us?

Friend, you were at one time the enemy of God (Colossians 1:21), and His hatred of your sin boiled over, but it didn't erupt on you, but instead on God's own Son. God made a feast for your soul in the cross of Christ (Luke 22:19-20). We now feed on the altar of the cross (Hebrews 13:10) and experience refreshment in the living water of the Holy Spirit (John 7:38-39).

Notice what this act of kindness and mercy, the preparing of food and drink for enemies, did to the king and country of Aram. It replaced anger with peace:

"So he prepared a great feast for them, and after they had finished eating and drinking, he sent them away, and they returned to their master. So the bands from Aram stopped raiding Israel's territory." 2 Kings 6:23 (NIV)

Application

Are you seething with anger today? Have you been mistreated by a parent, child, or colleague? Did your business partner, friend, or loved one betray you? Have your rights been violated? Pour out your angry heart to Jesus. He will hear you and answer you with His perfect peace. Come to the foot of the cross of Christ and remember that Jesus has not only paid your sin debt, but He has also paid for the sin that has produced such anger in your mind and heart. Jesus has carried your pain; He knows it. He is your Avenger. You can release your anger to Him and receive the healing that His wounds have purchased for you. Look to the cross of Christ and turn from angry outbursts and instead follow Christ in overcoming evil with good (Romans 12:21). This is how you can *"be angry and sin not"* (Ephesians 4:26).

Are you angry with God for allowing unwanted circumstances in your life? Are you frustrated because it seems nothing is going your way or because it appears that your offender has escaped punishment? Look to Jesus and remember the injustices He endured to secure your eternal joy. When you sinned against Jesus and failed to love and obey Him as you should, He did not abandon you, scream at you, or throw you out. He died in your place. He bore in His body all your sin, drank every drop of the cup of God's wrath against your sin, and paid the wages of your sin by dying in your place. You have escaped your eternal punishment because of Jesus.

These light momentary afflictions of your life are preparing for you an eternal weight of glory beyond all comparison (2 Corinthians 4:17). As you think of this eternal truth, the heat of your sinful anger will be replaced with refreshing joy and gratitude. How can you be angry with the God who loves you eternally and gave His only Son to redeem you?

> *"Do not let any unwholesome talk come out of your mouths, but only what is helpful for building others up according to their needs, that it may benefit those who listen. And do not grieve the Holy Spirit of God, with whom you were sealed for the day of redemption. Get rid of all bitterness, rage, and anger, brawling and slander, along with every form of malice. Be kind and compassionate to one another, forgiving each other, just as in Christ God forgave you." Ephesians 4:29-32*

Question: How can you look to Jesus and put away your anger today?

_____

_____

_____

_____

Looking to Jesus When Lonely

"My eyes are ever on the Lord, for only he will release my feet from the snare. Turn to me and be gracious to me, for I am lonely and afflicted." Psalm 25:15-16 NIV

We live in an age of ultra-connectedness through devices and communication applications of all kinds, and yet reports of loneliness are steadily rising. Studies and statistics abound from countries around the world, enlightening us about the adverse effects of loneliness on our minds and bodies. But when we are feeling the pain of loneliness, these facts are no comfort, only confirmation that we are not alone in our loneliness.

The evil one sees our loneliness and tempts us to self-comfort with food, immorality, drugs, and unhealthy relationships. Satan promises connection and fulfillment in our lifestyle choices, but he lies. Connecting with others around our temptations, our job, our love of food, beer, wine, or fashion, groups us but leaves us only wanting more.

The world tells us that what we need is a caring community, better friends, or professional therapy, but in the end, we find that people aren't the answer. Friends and family can surround us while our lives still feel empty, and our hearts are filled with longing to connect.

What we really want and need is to be fully known and fully loved, not for how we look, what we can do, or what we have, but for ourselves. However, in this fallen world of broken people, we will not find this type of fulfillment.

In Psalm 68, David sings praise to God because God protects and pursues those who are alone in the world. God puts these lonely ones in families and brings them into freedom and joy. Oh, friend, there is a remedy for our loneliness, and it is in looking to Jesus!

When Jesus went to the cross, He entered our loneliness, took it upon Himself. He experienced the ultimate loneliness by enduring the agony of separation from His Father so that we could experience eternal union with Him. Whereas before, we were those who were "disconnected from the Head" (Colossians 2:19), and this produced loneliness, now, in Jesus Christ, our Head (1 Corinthians 11:3), we are united forever with God.

> *In this life, we will feel lonely at times, but it is only a temporary feeling and never an actual reality for believers (Hebrews 13:5-6). In Jesus, we are fully known and fully loved (1 John 3:1). We belong in our eternal family (Luke 10:20), and Jesus loves us with an everlasting love from which we can never be separated (Romans 8:38-39). God's Holy Spirit fills and comforts us until we are face to face with our Beloved Jesus (John 14:26).*

Illustration

My God, my God, why have you forsaken Me?" Jesus cried out this verse from Psalm 22:1 when He was dying on the cross. We can feel the pain of His loneliness in these words.

Jesus Christ had come to this world, and the world did not recognize Him as their Creator but rejected Him (John 1:10-12). Jesus had come to His own, the Jewish nation, and they did not receive Him as the Messiah but instead hated Him. And at His last hour, Jesus' disciples all ran away from Him. Finally, on the cross, His Father had forsaken Him. He was alone.

Talk about lonely! There He hung between heaven and earth, rejected by God and man, forsaken by all. He had said earlier, through the prophet Isaiah, *"I have trodden the winepress alone; from the nations, no one was with me"* (Isaiah 63:3). Hanging on the cross, Jesus was utterly alone in the dark, alone as He bore the curse of the Law, alone as He suffered the wrath of God, alone as He paid for sin. No one was with Him. There was no relief for Him.

The reason He chose to enter this abject loneliness was to connect you forever with God; to unite the body and the Head. Jesus received rejection so that you could be accepted; He was forsaken so that you would be welcomed and embraced. He died lonely that you would forever live in the presence of God (2 Corinthians 4:14). Jesus rose victorious over loneliness. You have been raised with Him to a new life of fellowship with God and His people (1 John 1:7).

Application

Are you experiencing the pain of loneliness today? Are you feeling forgotten by friends, forsaken by the ones who are supposed to love you? Look to Jesus and see that He died on the cross and experienced utter loneliness in your place. He died alone so He could unite you with God and send His Spirit to always be with you. He rose to give you a new life of love and joy that is shared with people throughout time and around the world.

You are not alone, but you are loved! God has placed you in His family. Through His Son Jesus, God has qualified you to share in the inheritance of the saints in light. He has delivered you from the domain of darkness and transferred you to the kingdom of his beloved Son, in whom you have redemption, the forgiveness of sins (Colossians 1:12-14).

Embrace your feelings of loneliness as an invitation from Jesus to draw near to Him (James 4:8), to experience His love more deeply (Romans 5:1-8), to fellowship with Him in His sufferings (Philippians 3:10). Offer up the pain of your loneliness to Jesus and receive the comfort of His Spirit, for as you do, you will experience sweet intimacy with your Lord that will eclipse all your feelings of loneliness.

> **Question:** How does looking to Jesus' sacrificial death on the cross and His glorious resurrection bring relief from feelings of loneliness?

_____

_____

_____

_____

Day 22:

Looking to Jesus When Feeling Afraid

*"Fear not, for I am with you; be not dismayed, for I am
your God; I will strengthen you, I will help you, I will
uphold you with my righteous right hand." Isaiah 41:10*

*A*re you plagued with the fear of pain, disease, or dying? Have you shut
down under the weight of fearing failure, being misunderstood, or
rejected? Does the fear of punishment, judgment, or condemnation send you
running for cover? Or are you always on guard and ready to lash out at anyone
who seems threatening to you?

Fear can be a destructive tool of the enemy. We can know that Satan is
using fear to harm us when our fear fosters the deeds of the flesh in our lives.
*The acts of the flesh are obvious: sexual immorality, impurity, and debauchery;
idolatry and witchcraft; hatred, discord, jealousy, fits of rage, selfish ambition, dis-
sensions, factions, and envy; drunkenness, orgies, and the like.* Galatians 5:19-21

Scientists have labeled the human response to fear as "fight or flight." Fear
is visceral, instinctive, always disconcerting, but sometimes unwarranted. Do
you desire freedom from the control that fear has over your thinking and
actions? Look to Jesus!

The instruction to "fear not" is a frequently repeated call throughout Scripture, found in nearly every book of the Bible, first in Genesis 15:1 and last in
Revelation 1:17. So, we can infer that God not only anticipated His people's
fear but also that He made a plan to relieve our fears. The antidote to our fears
is looking to Jesus.

Alternatively, fear can be redeemed and used as a vehicle that drives us
to Jesus, our refuge. The book of Psalms is replete with expressions of fears

relieved by looking to and taking refuge in the Lord, such as *"God is our refuge and strength, a very present help in trouble. Therefore we will not fear though the earth gives way, though the mountains be moved into the heart of the sea, though its waters roar and foam, though the mountains tremble at its swelling."* Psalm 46:1-3

Whatever is inciting you toward fear is met today by Jesus with strength and victory! Look to Jesus for relief and hear Him say to you, *"Do not fear, only believe"* (Mark 5:36). Believe that Jesus died on the cross for you and has risen victorious for you. Believe that you were in Christ when He died and that in Him, you were raised to a new life of righteousness, which brings boldness (Proverbs 28:1). See Christ's perfect love displayed on Calvary and let this site cast out your fears (1 John 4:18). Remember, there is no punishment for you; death is defeated (Hebrews 2:14-15). You are safe in the shelter of the cross (Psalm 91:1-2)!

Illustration

As the Israelites were living in the Promised Land, they faced many battles. In one particular battle, they faced a massive army made up of warriors from Ammon, Moab, and Mt. Seir. They felt overpowered and underprepared for this attack. The king of the Jews, Jehoshaphat prayed to God and said,

> *"Our God, will you not judge them? For we have no power to face this vast army that is attacking us. We do not know what to do, but our eyes are on you." 2 Chronicles 20:12 (NIV)*

Sometimes we too can be paralyzed with fear. We don't know what to do or where to turn. We might feel that so many things are against us, that our thoughts overpower us, that we don't know how to handle situations. When you are afraid, feeling overpowered by a vast army that produces fear, look to Jesus. *"We don't know what to do, but our eyes are on you."* As you look to Jesus, you will see that He has made your battle His very own:

> *He said: "Listen, King Jehoshaphat and all who live in Judah and Jerusalem! This is what the Lord says to you: 'Do not be afraid or*

discouraged because of this vast army. For the battle is not yours, but God's." 2 Chronicles 20:15 (NIV)

"You will not have to fight this battle. Take up your positions; stand firm and see the deliverance the Lord will give you, Judah and Jerusalem. Do not be afraid; do not be discouraged. Go out to face them tomorrow, and the Lord will be with you.'" 2 Chronicles 20:17 (NIV)

See the cross as defeating your enemies, and bringing you to victory in all areas. See the resurrection of Jesus defeating even the last enemy, the enemy of death, and giving you eternal life. Look to Jesus when afraid, put faith in Him, and you, like Jehoshaphat and the Israelites, will lose your fear and win your battle. Praise the Lord for His victory won for you at Calvary, and do not fear.

"As they began to sing and praise, the Lord set ambushes against the men of Ammon and Moab and Mount Seir who were invading Judah, and they were defeated." 2 Chronicles 20:22 (NIV)

Application

Are you afraid of financial loss? Do you fear that someone will take advantage of you? Look to Jesus and see that He laid down His life for you. His death was to your advantage. See that though Jesus *"was rich, yet for your sake, he became poor so that you by His poverty might become rich"* (2 Corinthians 8:9). Out of the abundance that you have received from Jesus, bless others. Don't fear the loss of face or fortune; rejoice in the spiritual abundance that you have in Christ (Philippians 4;19)!

Do you hold back from serving or using your gifts afraid that others will mock or make fun of you? Look to Jesus and see Him willingly receiving the insults and abuse of all, not retaliating or shrinking back but entrusting Himself to the One who judges justly (1 Peter 2:23). Do not fear man, but look to Jesus and trust Him! What can man do to you that the wounds of Jesus cannot heal (1 Peter 2:24)?

Are you suffering from sleepless nights afraid of what tomorrow may bring? Look to Jesus, who has secured your eternal life by sacrificing His own. Look to Jesus, who has risen victorious and now sits at the right hand of the Father in heaven ever interceding for you. Set your heart and mind on Jesus, and He will give you rest.

In Psalm 3, King David's son, Absalom, was seeking to kill him, and so David prays through his fears in this way, *"O Lord, how many are my foes! Many are rising against me; many are saying of my soul," There is no salvation for him in God." Selah. But you, O Lord, are a shield about me, my glory, and the lifter of my head. I cried aloud to the Lord, and he answered me from his holy hill. Selah. I lay down and slept; I woke again, for the Lord sustained me. I will not be afraid..."*

God has answered you from His holy hill, too, dear friend. Look to Calvary's hill and see Jesus bowing His head and giving up His Spirit to lift your head. See Him giving up His Spirit so that you can be comforted in your distress. He is a shield around you; you are safe in Him.

Question: What fears are troubling you right now? Bring them to Jesus in prayer here:

_____

_____

_____

_____

Looking to Jesus When Empty

"Have this mind among yourselves, which is yours in Christ Jesus, who, though he was in the form of God, did not count equality with God a thing to be grasped, but emptied himself, by taking the form of a servant, being born in the likeness of men. And being found in human form, he humbled himself by becoming obedient to the point of death, even death on a cross." Philippians 2:5-8

*M*any people go through seasons of life where they feel empty, unfulfilled, flat, dull, hollow, or detached. Songwriters have described this feeling with the words, "Nothing really matters." So, we know the struggle with feeling empty is not uncommon, but it can be very disconcerting and even frightening.

For some people, emptiness is a long-standing feeling. They have always felt disconnected, as if something was missing, or like they have a void inside of them. Others are surprised by this feeling, usually after years of personal achievement and apparent success as with King Solomon, who wrote, *"Mean-ingless! Meaningless!" says the Teacher. "Utterly meaningless! Everything is meaningless"* (Ecclesiastes 1:2).

The world, our flesh, and the devil all continually reassure us that we can find satisfaction and fill the void ourselves; we only need more stuff, new stuff, better stuff. Or we need to work harder and achieve more so that we can go on better vacations and have more exciting experiences. And if that doesn't work, advertisements and billboards aplenty try to persuade us to try this pill or that pill to relieve our feelings of emptiness. Or if we don't like pills, we might consider the myriad of networks, stations, videos, and podcasts encouraging us to fill the void with more children, family, friends, ministry, activity, movies, music, food, alcohol, sports, sex, news, politics, fashion, or games. Sadly, while these things are not necessarily bad, if we seek to fill ourselves up with them, we will be left feeling disheartened, still wanting more, numb, and exhausted from the pursuit.

Dear friend, there is another way, a better way to address your feelings of emptiness! If you are feeling empty today, you can look to Jesus and be filled and satisfied in Him!

Perhaps you are thinking, "I believe in Jesus, but I still feel empty." Friend, there is a difference in merely believing (having head knowledge) and being filled with Christ. James wrote, *You believe that there is one God. Good! Even the demons believe that—and shudder.*" (James 2:19) As Christians, we don't merely believe in Jesus; He is our life (Colossians 3:4).

If you would be rid of your feelings of emptiness and experience the fullness that is in Christ, you've only to look to Jesus and behold His cross where He suffered for your sin, where He emptied Himself to fill you (Ephesians 3:19). Come and lift your heart to Him and receive all the love, life, healing, and wholeness that flows from Him.

Jesus went to the cross and emptied Himself completely so that you might receive the Holy Spirit (Galatians 3:14) and everything you need for life and godliness (2 Peter 1:3). He poured out His life to fill yours up with His amazing love (1 John 3:1), abundant joy (1 Peter 1:8), and peace that passes understanding (Philippians 4:7).

Illustration

A woman by the name of Naomi left Bethlehem with her family during a famine; they traveled to the country of Moab. They went on what was supposed to be a temporary "sojourn" (a short stay) and ended up staying ten years, during which time Naomi's husband and two sons died (Ruth 1:1-5).

Naomi then heard the good news that God had come to the aid of His people in Bethlehem by providing food for them, so Naomi returned to Bethlehem with her daughter-in-law, Ruth. But it was a bittersweet homecoming for Naomi; she had lost everything dear to her - her husband and sons. She was empty and hurting (Ruth 1:19-22).

"When the people of Bethlehem saw Naomi again, they said, "Could this be Naomi?" She replied, "Don't call me Naomi," she told them. "Call me Mara, because the Almighty has made my life very bitter. I went away full, but the Lord has brought me back empty" (Ruth 1:20-21).

God used Naomi's feelings of emptiness to draw her back home to Israel. And then God took Naomi from empty and bitter to happy and full through a "Kinsman-Redeemer" from Bethlehem by the name of Boaz. Boaz was a close relative of Naomi, who was not only wealthy and full of love, but also willing to redeem and marry Naomi's Moabite daughter-in-law, Ruth. In the end, Ruth gives birth to a son, and Naomi's joy is restored in full (Ruth 4:13-17, Luke 3:32).

Dear friend, to turn from the Lord and go out into the world is a deliberate choice for emptiness and dissatisfaction. It leaves us disillusioned, sad, bitter, and empty.

If you are hurting with feelings of emptiness today, you also have a Redeemer from Bethlehem named Jesus. He is a man of great wealth, who deliberately became poor for you on the cross that you would become rich (2 Corinthians 8:9). Jesus gave up all of Himself for you at the cross to fill you by His Spirit because He loves to take empty people and make them full.

"For in Christ all the fullness of the Deity lives in bodily form, and in Christ, you have been brought to fullness. He is the head over every power and authority." Colossians 2:9-10 (NIV)

Application

Are you feeling like Naomi today? Have your life's losses been so significant that you think there is nothing left for you here? Do you feel empty and bitter about your situation? Look to Jesus! Receive His invitation to come home to Your Redeemer and be filled with the good and eternal things that He provides (Luke 1:53). Lift your empty heart to Him and wait; at the proper time, He will fill you to overflowing (Psalm 23:5).

Are you lacking purpose and asking yourself, "What's the point?" Do you feel that your endeavors are meaningless? Does everything disappoint and leave you wanting? Turn from your empty cisterns (Jeremiah 2:13) and look to Jesus, your fountain of life (Psalm 36:8-9).

Take time to be still and fix your eyes, your heart, and your thoughts on Jesus right now. See Him taking your emptiness upon Himself, see Him bearing the weight of your pain. See Him all alone, emptying Himself for you, dying your death. See him thirsting and enduring the agony of eternal craving so that you might experience fullness and liberty in Him. He abandoned all for you - His royalty, His rights, His freedom, His life, and His Spirit - so that you would be filled with His Spirit, His love, His wisdom, and His life (Colossians 1:9, Ephesians 1:23, Ephesians 3:19).

Oh, friend, Jesus is your Good Shepherd! He has laid down His life so that you will not be empty and wanting (Psalm 23:1) but rather seated at His table, feasting with your cup overflowing (Psalm 23:5). When feelings of emptiness intrude, look to Jesus and remember His body broken for you and His blood poured out for you, for as you do, you will experience His Holy Spirit pouring love into your heart (Romans 5:5) and filling you so that you can sing with the psalmist:

"Because your love is better than life, my lips will glorify you. I will praise you as long as I live, and in your name, I will lift up my hands. I will be fully satisfied as with the richest of foods; with singing lips, my mouth will praise you. On my bed I remember you; I think of you through the watches of the night. Because you are my help, I sing in the shadow of your wings. I cling to you; your right hand upholds me." Psalm 63:3-8

Question: How does it fill your heart when you look at Jesus emptying Himself on the cross for you?

_____

_____

_____

_____

DAY 24:

Looking to Jesus When Your Heart is Hard

*"For he is our God, and we are the people of his pasture
and the sheep of his hand. Today, if you hear his voice,
do not harden your hearts..." Psalm 95:7-8*

When we think of a hard heart, we might initially get visions of criminals or terrorists, people who are belligerent and oblivious to the needs of others. But hard hearts happen to Christians too.

Think about it. Have you ever experienced a time where you felt unresponsive to God's Word? You read your Bible, but it just seems like words on a page because you aren't getting anything out of it. Maybe you even find yourself ignoring your Bible and neglecting your prayer time altogether. Your heart is hard, and you've forgotten Christ's sacrifice to purchase you.

Or maybe you go to church, you sit, stand, and even sing at all the appropriate times, but you are not engaged at all; your mind is a million miles away. You think you've heard it all before. You believe the gospel message is for salvation but not relevant to your daily life. You hide or minimize your sins while judging others harshly, holding onto bitterness, nursing grudges, lashing out in anger, and refusing to forgive. Your heart is hard; you've forgotten the great debt of sin that Christ paid off for you with His death on the cross.

Or perhaps temptation comes to you, but instead of taking the way out that God provides through Jesus' death and resurrection, you shut your ears to the voice of the Spirit. You turn from the cross of Christ and choose to go your own way, indulging the cravings of your flesh as if you were alive to sin and dead to God. You think you deserve a treat. You are frustrated with God, thinking He isn't meeting your needs. You covet what others have and complain about what you don't have. Unbelief has hardened your heart.

But what are we to do when we realize that our heart is hard? Is there a remedy for this dreadful malady? Yes! Look to Jesus! The gospel, the great news of the atoning death and victorious resurrection of Jesus, is the only softening agent for a hard heart.

Much as bread goes stale and hardens when it is left out and unprotected, if we do not daily cover our hearts and protect our minds with the redeeming work of Jesus on the cross, sin will increase in our lives, and our hearts will grow hard. But if we come to Jesus and wash in the blood of His new covenant, then our hearts will be softened anew.

When we look to Jesus crucified, He opens our eyes and reveals Himself to us in His Word. As we hear again, the good news of our forgiveness that flows to us from Calvary, our ears become receptive to the voice of the Spirit. As we consider the humility of Christ, the Lamb of God, dying our death, our minds are renewed and transformed by Christ. As we behold the empty tomb of Jesus, unbelief is banished, and the joy of our salvation is restored (1 Corinthians 11:23-26, Luke 7:22, Romans 12:2, Hebrews 2:9, Hebrews 12:1-3).

Illustration

In the book of Exodus, we read how the Israelites were saved from God's wrath through the death of the Passover Lamb, were "baptized" at the Red Sea, and then lived for over forty years in the wilderness under the leadership of Moses. At one point on their journey, they came to a place where there was no water to drink, so they complained to Moses, murmured against God, and "put the Lord to the test" (Exodus 17:2).

Psalm 95:8 tells us the reason they were complaining and murmuring: they had hard hearts. "*Do not harden your hearts as you did at Meribah, as you did that day at Massah in the wilderness, where your ancestors tested me; they tried me, though they had seen what I did.*" Psalms 95:8-9 (NIV)

What was the solution that God provided to these hard-hearted complainers?

"*I will stand there before you by the rock at Horeb. Strike the rock, and water will come out of it for the people to drink.*" So Moses did this in the sight of the elders of Israel." Exodus 17:6 (NIV)

God told Moses to strike a rock, and out of it came water for the people. What a unique solution! We might consider digging for water but probably wouldn't think of striking a rock for it. 1 Corinthians 10:4 provides this commentary:

"They all ate the same spiritual food and drank the same spiritual drink; for they drank from the spiritual rock that accompanied them, and that rock was Christ." 1 Corinthians 10:3-4 (NIV)

Ah, now we understand! The struck rock pointed forward to Christ, who was hung on the cross and struck to death for us. And from His death flows the river of the Holy Spirit, the Living Water, who meets all our needs.

What is the solution for a hard heart? It is to look to Jesus, see Him being struck and wounded for you, see Him lifted up to die, receive the Holy Spirit by faith, and drink deeply of the waters of life!

Like the Israelites, we have been saved and baptized, and are now living our daily lives under God's leadership. But when times get hard, we might start to think that the message of the cross is no longer relevant. We might think we need something new or more than the gospel. And this is one of the errors that can foster a hard heart - believing that the message of the cross is merely for salvation and not for everyday life.

But the message of the cross is not merely the message of salvation; it is the message of transformation. We are to look daily, to see the Lamb of God who takes away the sin of the world, to find fresh living water every day at the foot of the cross. There, Jesus was crucified to put your sins to death; at the cross, your record of wrongs, that legal document that was against you, was nailed into the flesh of Jesus, where it was permanently removed from you (Colossians 2:14).

Application

Do you feel distant from Jesus today? Have the difficult circumstances of your life eclipsed the wonder of the cross of Christ for you? Has your time with the Lord fallen by the way? Is your faith stale? Have you fallen into a pattern of habitual sin and been hardened by it?

Oh, dear friend, come to the cross of Christ and let it strike your hard heart, let it wound you and heal you, let it raise you up and give you relief. Let the water and blood that flows from Jesus' wounded side wash over and refresh you today. Remember God's goodness to you in taking you out of the dominion of darkness and bringing you into the kingdom of His beloved Son, Jesus (Colossians 1:13).

Consider the wounds of Christ:

A crown of thorns pierced His head so that your mind might be renewed and transformed.

His back was struck and shredded to atone for your sins and to heal your heart wounds.

His beard was plucked out; His face was struck; His hands and feet were pierced to pay for the wicked things that you have said and done.

He hung naked and exposed in your sin and shame so that you could be clothed with His righteousness.

His heart was pierced to save and sanctify yours. *"I am poured out like water, and all my bones are out of joint; my heart is like wax; it is melted within my breast"* Psalm 22:14.

He breathed out His last and gave up His Spirit to fill you and secure your eternal life.

Come and remember that you are loved, dear friend. Your sins are forgiven. There is abundant life for you in Jesus. Be comforted by the cross today. Let the water of the Spirit and the blood of Christ restore your heart today.

> *"See to it, brothers and sisters, that none of you has a sinful, unbelieving heart that turns away from the living God. But encourage one another daily, as long as it is called "Today," so that none of you may be hardened by sin's deceitfulness." Hebrews 3:12-13 (NIV)*

Question: How does looking at the cross of Christ soften your heart?

_____

_____

_____

_____

Looking to Jesus When Feeling Weary

"As for you, brothers, do not grow weary in doing good." 2 Thessalonians 3:13

$\mathcal{E}$xhausted, depleted, spent, bushed, fatigued, sapped, knackered, or beat; whatever you call it, feeling weary is part of the human experience. The specific things that wear us out vary, but there are commonalities.

First, we have the physical weariness of life. Work of any kind creates a longing in us for rest: parents desire uninterrupted sleep, employees, and business owners alike long for a vacation, caregivers wish for a break, students eagerly anticipate holidays. Our bodies are frail and need physical rest. And if we neglect this need, our bodies will eventually shut down. The need for physical rest is an inescapable fact of life.

Then there is spiritual and emotional fatigue, which comes from the constant barrage of struggles in ourselves, our families, our communities, and our countries. We get worn out by wrestling with our flesh and bumping up against other people's flesh. Time and time again, our feelings are trampled, our hopes dashed, our spirits depressed by our own failures and the failures of others. This weariness is so severe that we cannot vacation our way out of it. We need a Savior, a Comforter, a Rest-Giver.

In Matthew 11, we read Jesus' invitation to all who are spiritually and emotionally weary, *"Come to me, all who labor and are heavy laden, and I will give you rest. Take my yoke upon you and learn from me, for I am gentle and lowly in heart, and you will find rest for your souls. For my yoke is easy, and my burden is light."* Matthew 11:28-30

Indeed, Jesus is the answer for the weary, sin-ladened, law-burdened heart. We cannot fix ourselves. We cannot achieve lasting victory over our sin struggles or face the sin struggles of others apart from Jesus and His cross. As we come to the cross of Christ to have our sin burdens lifted, and to receive the sacrificial love of God, it both transforms our hearts and gives us rest. We look to our Lord, risen and victorious, and receive His Spirit and His power, which comforts and heals us and gives us new life.

But there is another type of tiredness that threatens us after we find rest from our law-keeping labors in Jesus' death and resurrection for us, and this is the weariness of doing what is right. This weariness comes to those in full-time ministry and volunteers, to pastors and nursery workers, the young and the old. It can come on gradually or suddenly, but this temptation, this being weary in well-doing, comes to the whole body of Christ at some point in time. So, what are we to do when our *"doing good"* for the glory of God becomes "Good grief, when does it end?" We look to Jesus!

We find this solution in Hebrews 12:3, *"Consider him who endured from sinners such hostility against himself, so that you may not grow weary or faint-hearted."* There is nothing more encouraging and empowering to the heart than looking to the cross of Christ and seeing the lengths that Jesus went to find us, rescue us, and give us rest. He pushed past His weariness in the Garden of Gethsemane to go to the cross, to provide rest for you.

Illustration

In Exodus 17, we read of a particular battle between the Israelites and the Amalekites in the valley of Rephidim. Joshua led the soldiers into war and Moses took two others, Aaron and Hur, and went to the top of a hill to intercede for the fighting soldiers in the valley below:

> *"So Joshua fought the Amalekites as Moses had ordered, and Moses, Aaron, and Hur went to the top of the hill." Exodus 17:10 (NIV)*

God made the outcome of this battle dependant on what Moses did on the hill, whether he lifted his arms up or not, rather than on the keen strategizing or the strength of the fighting soldiers:

"As long as Moses held up his hands, the Israelites were winning,
but whenever he lowered his hands, the Amalekites were winning."
Exodus 17:11 (NIV)

You can imagine the fighting soldiers becoming weary in the battle, growing tired and losing their strength, but as they turned and looked up and saw those three men on the hill, the one in the middle with his arms upraised in victory, they fought on all the more.

But Moses got weary in the battle, too. His arms grew tired, so he needed his brothers to help him:

"When Moses' hands grew tired, they took a stone and put it under
him, and he sat on it. Aaron and Hur held his hands up—one on
one side, one on the other—so that his hands remained steady
till sunset." Exodus 17:12 (NIV)

This story teaches us two important things:

When we become weary in the battle, or if we get tired in ministry, we can turn to the hill of Calvary and see three men on a hill, and the One in the middle has His hands upraised in victory. This sight of our victorious Savior will renew our energy and give us strength for the day.

When we become weary in doing good, when our arms droop from exhaustion, we must allow our brothers and sisters to come alongside us and encourage us to look to the cross, upholding our weary arms. The body of Christ is admonished to *"strengthen the feeble hands, steady the knees that give way; say to those with fearful hearts, "Be strong, do not fear; your God will come...he will come to save you"* (Isaiah 35:3-4). And He has come to save us in the person of Jesus, and we strengthen ourselves and each other as we look to Him.

"So Joshua overcame the Amalekite army with the sword." Exodus
17:13 (NIV)

Moses was relieved and encouraged to have Aaron and Hur to support him in his ministry. And the Israelite soldiers were strengthened and energized to look up to the hill and see the man in the middle with his hands lifted high proclaiming their victory. Similarly, when we feel the weariness of doing what is right intruding, we can turn our eyes to Calvary and see that Jesus *"disarmed the powers and authorities, he made a public spectacle of them, triumphing over them by the cross"* (Colossians 2:15).

Application

Are you a tired parent, weary of training your children in righteousness? Or a prayer warrior, who is feeling all prayed out? Or a worship leader who is feeling flat? Maybe you are just weary of forgiving those who sin against you again and again, or perhaps you are tired of supporting that friend who keeps falling into sin traps. Maybe you are feeling sick of speaking the truth in love when it feels like no one is listening. Oh, friend, if you are feeling drained from doing what is good, look to Jesus!

Look to the hill of Calvary and see Jesus winning the battle for you! Consider Jesus and how He poured out all His strength and His Spirit so that His Spirit would fill and fortify you. Remember that Jesus, as your Mediator, endured to the end. He sacrificed His life to save and sanctify you. His victory is yours; He is *"the founder and perfecter"* of your faith. Look to Jesus and receive His resurrection power that will not only raise you on the last day but every day!

Do you see someone doing what is right, but their enthusiasm for the work has waned? Come alongside them, help them to rest on Jesus, their Rock, and then prop up their arms with the good news of Christ's death and resurrection. In so doing, you will strengthen and steady them along the way!

> *"And let us not grow weary of doing good, for in due season we will reap, if we do not give up. So then, as we have opportunity, let us do good to everyone, and especially to those who are of the household of faith." Galatians 6:9-10*

Question: How does looking to Jesus revive you today?

_____

_____

_____

_____

Looking to Jesus When Suffering

"Therefore, since we have been justified by faith, we have peace with God through our Lord Jesus Christ. Through him, we have also obtained access by faith into this grace in which we stand, and we rejoice in hope of the glory of God. Not only that, but we rejoice in our sufferings, knowing that suffering produces endurance, and endurance produces character, and character produces hope, and hope does not put us to shame, because God's love has been poured into our hearts through the Holy Spirit who has been given to us." Romans 5:1-5

When sin entered the world, suffering came with it. Physical pain, mental anguish, emotional distress, and spiritual torment have continued throughout time. We see it every day in the form of illness, accidents, disasters, abuse, broken relationships, betrayal, guilt, shame, etc.

As a rule, the world and our flesh abhor suffering; many see it as senseless and believe if it can't be avoided then it should be medicated with "comfort food," alcohol, sweets, prescription medications, illegal drugs, "me time," or any other activity or substance that distracts from discomfort.

And while there is certainly nothing wrong with alleviating suffering, as believers in Jesus, we harm ourselves and miss out on the blessings God has for us when we try to manage our suffering (or others' suffering) apart from the cross of Christ. Turning to false Saviors (food, drugs, sex, self, etc.) in our pain, compounds our suffering, but looking to Jesus relieves it.

When we look to Jesus, we see God is not aloof to our pain. He has entered into it in the Person of Jesus. When we look at the cross, we see Jesus entering into our pain. The prophet Isaiah put it this way, *"He was despised and rejected by mankind, a man of suffering, and familiar with pain. Like one from whom people hide their faces he was despised, and we held him in low esteem. Surely he took up our pain and bore our suffering, yet we considered him punished by God, stricken by him, and afflicted. But he was pierced for our transgressions; he was crushed for our iniquities; the punishment that brought us peace was on him, and by his wounds, we are healed." Isaiah 53:3-5 NIV*

Suffering of any kind hurts. It is agony. Look at all the words used to describe Christ's suffering - despised, rejected, devalued, pain, stricken, afflicted, pierced, crushed, wounded, etc. As with Jesus, our pain is real; we don't want to deny it, but we do want to look to Jesus so that He can redeem it.

Oh, dear friend, in the suffering of Christ on the cross, we see the power and glory of God (John 7:39, Romans 1:16-17, Hebrews 1:3)! Similarly, when we look to Jesus in our weaknesses and our sufferings, God is glorified, and His power revealed in us.

When we are suffering, and we look to Christ and draw near to Him with our pain, we experience deep intimacy with Him. His sacrificial love pours into our hearts by His life-giving Spirit to comfort and encourage us, and His resurrection power flows through us to sustain us as we wait for the redemption of all things (Romans 8:22-24).

Illustration

In the Old Testament, one man stands out as having suffered a lot - Job. In one day, all of Job's children died, he lost his livelihood of flocks and herds, his house, and all his wealth. Shortly after that, he lost his physical health so that he had nothing left except a distraught wife who told him to "curse God and die." It is shocking in its severity.

What can sustain a man through this kind of unrelenting suffering? What can take you and I through very difficult times of suffering?

We get the answer to those questions when we come to Job 19:

> *"I know that my redeemer lives, and that in the end he will stand*
> *on the earth. And after my skin has been destroyed, yet in my*

flesh I will see God; I myself will see him with my own eyes—I, and not another. How my heart yearns within me!" Job 19:25-27

Job was focused on His Redeemer, and so Job says the following things:

> *My Redeemer lives (Job 19:25).*
> *My Redeemer is God (Job 19:26).*
> *My heart yearns to see God (Job 19:27).*

A "redeemer" is one who gains or regains possession of something in exchange for payment. Job knew He had a Redeemer, Someone who would purchase and regain him through a great payment. Perhaps, Job supernaturally understood that the payment to redeem him was connected with the suffering of the coming Messiah, as foretold in Genesis 3:15.

And yet, Job knew this Redeemer lives. So Job knew there would be a redemption price paid, and there would be a living Redeemer. Job saw in a concealed form, the gospel of Jesus Christ: God, His Redeemer, would pay the price for Job's redemption, and then He would live forevermore.

Job derived great comfort during his suffering by focusing on His Redeemer, looking to Jesus. Job believed that he would see His Redeemer (Jesus) in the end, and this made Job's heart yearn to be with Him.

Dear friend, what is it that will enable you to endure great suffering and find real comfort in the midst of it? Look to Jesus, who, at the price of His own life, bought you back for God. "*And they sang a new song, saying: "You are worthy to take the scroll and to open its seals because you were slain, and with your blood you purchased for God persons from every tribe and language and people and nation*" (Revelation 5:9).

And not only did He purchase you back (redeem you) from sin through His death on the cross, He rose from the dead on the third day. Your Redeemer lives! Let that stoke a fire in your heart, causing you to yearn for the day you will see His face. One day soon, you will experience an embrace by the God with pierced hands.

Application

Are you suffering in your heart, mind, or body today? Are you growing tired or discouraged in the face of your suffering? Maybe you are dealing with an illness or feeling the anguish of loss today. Whatever the source or type of discomfort you are feeling, you can look to Christ for relief. He is the One who can sustain you!

You cannot sustain yourself, and you shouldn't even try! Instead, Jesus calls you to bring your loss, your pain, and your anguish to the foot of His cross. He invites you to come to Him with your grief, your sadness, and your confusion. And as you do, Jesus' resurrection power flows out to you, and He sustains you by His amazing grace so that you can say, *"But he said to me, "My grace is sufficient for you, for my power is made perfect in weakness." Therefore I will boast all the more gladly of my weaknesses, so that the power of Christ may rest upon me. For the sake of Christ, then, I am content with weaknesses, insults, hardships, persecutions, and calamities. For when I am weak, then I am strong."* 2 Corinthians 12:9-10

As Jesus carries you through your time of suffering, others will see your weakness and suffering and wonder about the hope that you have through it. And you'll have a chance to tell them the good news of Christ's death and resurrection that is powerful for salvation and sanctification (1 Peter 3:15) and enables you to endure the worst kind of suffering. Suffering is hard, but it is productive and evangelistic when we look to Jesus through our tears.

> *"That I may know him and the power of his resurrection, and may share his sufferings, becoming like him in his death"* (Philippians 3:10).

Question: How does looking to Jesus sustain you through suffering?

_____

_____

_____

_____

Looking to Jesus When Doubting

"And a great windstorm arose, and the waves were break-ing into the boat so that the boat was already filling. But he was in the stern, asleep on the cushion. And they woke him and said to him, "Teacher, do you not care that we are perishing?" And he awoke and rebuked the wind and said to the sea, "Peace! Be still!" And the wind ceased, and there was a great calm. He said to them, "Why are you so afraid? Have you still no faith?" Mark 4:37-40

Sometimes in life, we come up against struggles or trials that are so difficult we feel we might not survive them, or death seems preferable to living through them. Perhaps we get the news that due to a lost job or a failed invest-ment, we are in financial ruin. Or an incurable disease strikes us or someone that we love. Maybe a friend or family member dies through a sudden accident or by violence. Or most commonly, a loved one or we are caught in a sin trap (drunkenness, sexual impurity, gluttony, etc.) from which there seems to be no escape.

Uncertainty and doubts naturally surface and trouble us in difficult times. Some will doubt that God even exists, while others will get stuck on doubting God's goodness or love.

Looking to Jesus and His wounds dispel these fears, showing us that the worst thing that could ever happen to a human being, death on a cross, was followed by a powerful resurrection from the dead. The cross of Christ and the empty tomb bring comfort to us who need reassurance that God is real, loving, and kind. God came in the Person of Jesus and lived with and for us, died sacrificially, and rose victorious. He is even now preparing a place for us. When we doubt God, we can look to the cross of Christ for the restoration of our faith and joy.

But there is another more insidious doubt that threatens the faith of believers when the struggles of life are weighty, and that is that Christ, His death and resurrection, are insufficient (even irrelevant) to the current difficulty.

The tempting thought is that we need Jesus plus something. The "something" we think we need could be anything - a bank account with money, a cure for our illness, justice for the wrongs against us, an apology, a supportive spouse, loving children, the removal of our difficulty, etc. And while asking God for these things is appropriate and right, we must guard our hearts against the lie of Satan that we cannot experience freedom in Christ or live in righteousness if God answers us with a "no" or "not now."

About his own discouraging and frustrating struggle, the Apostle Paul prayed, *"Three times I pleaded with the Lord about this, that it should leave me. But he said to me, "My grace is sufficient for you, for my power is made perfect in weakness." Therefore I will boast all the more gladly of my weaknesses, so that the power of Christ may rest upon me. For the sake of Christ, then, I am content with weaknesses, insults, hardships, persecutions, and calamities. For when I am weak, then I am strong." 2 Corinthians 12:8-10*

Many Christians have wrongly relegated the sufficiency of the cross of Christ to their eternal salvation, and so they continue to struggle, stumble, and fall in their daily walk. They run here and there, seeking a new solution. But God promises that His grace poured out to us from the cross of Christ is sufficient not only for our salvation but also for our sanctification. We are to look to the cross every day of our lives until the end. For when we do, we find that the blood of Jesus not only saves us from the penalty of sin but also sets us free from the power of sin (1 Peter 1:14-19, Romans 6:18)!

Looking to Jesus, considering all that He endured on the cross, is the way to relieve your doubts about the sufficiency of Christ for the troublesome struggles of your life (Mark 4:35-41, John 8:36). As you look past your storm to see your Savior, you will experience His peace, and your doubts will dissipate. In your sin trap, look up to Jesus and see His nail-pierced hands reaching down to pull you up and out, and you will experience the grace of God, which will teach you to say no to your flesh and yes to walking by the Spirit. Oh, friend, whatever your difficulty, Jesus is enough!

Illustration

"But immediately, Jesus spoke to them, saying, "Take heart; it is I. Do not be afraid." And Peter answered him, "Lord, if it is you, command me to come to you on the water." He said, "Come." So Peter got out of the boat and walked on the water and came to Jesus." Matthew 14: 27-29

In Matthew 14, we read the account of the disciples out in their boat late at night in the middle of a storm. At some point, Jesus goes walking out to them on water, but instead of being comforted, they are all terrified. Jesus calls out to them to reassure them, but Peter, somewhat doubtful, responds to Jesus with an *"If it is you..."* request. And Jesus calls Peter to come to Him out on the water. Peter's doubts fall away! With his eyes fixed on Jesus, Peter stepped out of the boat and supernaturally walked on water in the middle of a storm.

"But when he saw the wind, he was afraid, and beginning to sink he cried out, "Lord, save me." Matthew 14:30

Everything was good until Peter became distracted. He stopped looking at Jesus and began to focus on the storm. Amidst the wind and the waves, Peter's doubts resurfaced and overcame him; He looked away from Jesus and began to sink! With his attention diverted from Jesus, Peter could no longer walk supernaturally but only sink as any person would do.

Peter believed in the power of Jesus, initially. In faith, Peter stepped out of the boat and walked on top of the water, but then he doubted Jesus' ability to keep him afloat, and down Peter went.

The good news is that Jesus did not abandon Peter in his time of need. Peter cried out, "Lord, save me!" and *Jesus immediately reached out his hand and took hold of him, saying to him, "O you of little faith, why did you doubt?"* Matthew 14:31

Application

For a moment, compare Peter's story with your own.

At some point, like Peter, you heard the call of Jesus and responded in obedience. You looked to Jesus and ventured out into the unknown waters of faith. You believed Jesus' Word, trusted what He said to you, and you were so fixated on Him that you were living a life of confidence in Christ and overcoming sin as you walked by faith.

But then a difficulty or struggle came to you that was discouraging and distracting. Maybe it was an illness, a financial loss, an inability to lose weight, a wayward child, something so big in your mind that it eclipsed the power of Jesus Christ. You began to focus on that problem, and doubts surfaced. Now, you find that you keep sinking under the weight of those doubts. What is wrong here?

You initially looked to Christ for deliverance from God's wrath and salvation from hell, and you believed in the power of the cross to make you right with God, but now, your difficulty has you doubting! You've stopped looking to Jesus, and instead, now all you see is the problem you are trying to overcome. Maybe you've turned to many of this world's solutions and have been repeatedly disappointed.

The remedy is to see Jesus! Specifically, look at the cross and see Jesus dying to set you free from the power of your problem. See His wounds and stripes as He took your punishment, see His death as He paid your penalty! Then see Him rising from the dead, having defeated the devil and death, and having overcome the world. See Him at the right hand of the Father, justifying you, interceding for you. Fixate on Jesus! See His power? See His love? He is the Lion of the tribe of Judah, and He has overcome, and now His love and power both reside in you, dear friend.

Maybe it's time for you to say to Jesus right now what Peter shouted when he was sinking in the waves: "Lord, save me!" Shake off your doubt and look to Jesus! View His loving cross, see His shed blood, hear His cry, "It is finished," and trust His power not only to save you from wrath but to break the power of sin in your life and speak peace to your storm, if you look to Jesus and the power of His cross and resurrection.

"Commit your way to the Lord; trust in him, and he will act."
Psalm 37:5

Question: How does putting faith in the gospel alleviate your doubts and enable you to be an overcomer in all things?

_____

_____

_____

_____

DAY 28:

Looking to Jesus When in Conflict

"What causes quarrels, and what causes fights among you? Is it not this, that your passions are at war within you? You desire and do not have, so you murder. You covet and cannot obtain, so you fight and quarrel. You do not have because you do not ask." James 4:1-2

Conflict of some kind is ever-present in our lives. Global, civil, political, and environmental disagreements confront us daily. In our communities, disputes abound regarding education, growth and development, and social concerns. Church history is replete with quarrels over issues like baptism, salvation, and eschatology. In our homes, discord is frequent between siblings, parents and children, spouses, or roommates. Conflict is inescapable because it resides even in our own minds; we argue with ourselves regularly.

When arguments arise, we all have a default position. Some of us get aggressive, we step up to the challenge, and we don't back down. We argue passionately, and often win the battle but lose the war. Others of us try to avoid conflict at all costs. We remain silent and suppress our feelings. We would rather forfeit and retreat than prolong the discomfort of the disagreement. And some of us will vacillate between aggression and passivity, depending on the topic at hand.

We are so familiar with conflict that it is easy to disconnect it from our faith in Jesus Christ. We might reason, "Sure, I believe in Jesus. I love God's amazing grace, but what's that got to do with politics, my irritating neighbor, or my child who is challenging me on everything?"

But the truth is that conflict of any kind is meant to be an excellent back-drop for the diamond of the gospel. We must look to Jesus, especially when disagreements arise because it is through Him that true peace and reconciliation can be achieved.

Christ's death and resurrection to save us is the great unifier for believers. Jesus' finished work on the cross allows us to interact with each other in humility because we know we were all born equally sinners in need of a Savior (Philippians 2:3-10). Looking to Jesus first, when conflict arises, gives us the eternal perspective we need to respond to one another in love (1 Timothy 1:5) and to be a light to our world (Matthew 5:14, John 13:35).

On the other hand, when we engage in arguments but ignore the cross of Christ (1 Corinthians 1:18), we miss the opportunity for grace to abound to us and those around us (Romans 5:20). When we attempt to navigate conflict according to our own understanding, we deny the power of the cross and set ourselves up for destruction (Proverbs 3:5-6, Galatians 5:15).

> *"For in him all the fullness of God was pleased to dwell, 20 and through him to reconcile to himself all things, whether on earth or in heaven, making peace by the blood of his cross." Colossians 1:19-20*

In Colossians 1:20, we learn that Christ's shed blood on the cross is what brought peace between God and man. Now we must *"continue in the faith, stable and steadfast, not shifting from the hope of the gospel"* and trust that if the cross of Christ can bring peace to the eternal conflict between God and us, then it will also bring peace in our temporary conflicts with one another.

> *"For he himself is our peace, who has made us both one and has broken down in his flesh the dividing wall of hostility by abolishing the law of commandments expressed in ordinances, that he might create in himself one new man in place of the two, so making peace, and might reconcile us both to God in one body through the cross, thereby killing the hostility." Ephesians 2:14-16*

Illustration

"I appeal to you, brothers, by the name of our Lord Jesus Christ, that all of you agree, and that there be no divisions among you, but that you be united in the same mind and the same judgment. For it has been reported to me by Chloe's people that there is quarreling among you, my brothers." 1 Corinthians 1:10-11

In the Corinthian church, there was quarreling and division. People were at odds over who they thought was the best teacher, who they should follow, whose gifts were more significant, etc.

When it came to addressing this division and quarreling, Paul does something beautiful and productive: he runs right to the cross of Jesus! He gets their attention and redirects them to Christ and His death on the cross so that they might be humbled. As their vision is captured by the cross, they remember that they are loved, and when they look to Jesus, they will be able to *"agree"* and have *"no divisions."*

Now notice how Paul guides the Corinthians to the cross of Christ. He asks some rhetorical questions and makes a definitive statement:

Rhetorical questions: *"Is Christ divided? Was Paul crucified for you?"* (1 Corinthians 1:13). If Christ was not divided, neither should His body be, and the way to avoid it is by the quarreling parties coming to the cross together. When Paul asks, *"Was Paul crucified for you?"* he is asking them to remember and consider Jesus' death on the cross, which unifies them (John 17:22-23), teaching them to follow Jesus, who died for them.

Definitive statement: *"For I decided that while I was with you I would forget everything except Jesus Christ, the one who was crucified"* (1 Corinthians 2:2).

Here Paul is driving home the main theme of Scripture, Jesus Christ, and Him crucified. He was teaching the Corinthians that everything, including their disagreements were to be subject to the gospel.

Application

Are you embroiled in conflict today? Are you trying to manage your situation based on your own understanding and frustrated because resolution seems to evade you at every turn? Look to Jesus!

The shed blood of Jesus on the cross is the power of God for reconciliation. As believers, we are to be *"looking to Jesus"* in all things (Hebrews 12:2), including conflict.

Jesus set his face determinedly toward Jerusalem, to the great battle of Calvary, where He would rescue us from our most significant conflict, eternal separation from God caused by the rebellion of our sin against Him. He will not abandon us to our own devices now.

As believers, reconciled to God through Jesus' death and resurrection for us, we want to follow Him, empowered by His Spirit, controlled by His love, to navigate conflict in the shadow of His cross, looking past the discomfort of our disagreements to the hope of a joyful reconciliation.

When conflict comes, look to Jesus first! Before you tweet about your political preferences or get on your soapbox about some community issue, look to the cross and ask, "Does what I am about to say communicate gospel love?"

When your neighbor is irritating you, look to Jesus! At the foot of His cross, look up and see the crown of thorns on Jesus' head, His nail-pierced hands and feet, and, in light of the love of Jesus and the forgiveness you have generously received, think of a way to bless your neighbor.

When your child challenges your authority, don't get into a screaming match as the world does. Instead, look to Jesus! See Him dying for you while you were still rebellious, and then in light of the great kindness that Jesus has shown you, let your kindness lead your child to repentance (Romans 2:4). Assure your child that they are loved and gently guide them in grace to Jesus.

Let us not live according to the flesh by trying to ignore or living to incite conflict, but instead, let us look to the cross of Christ and remember that His blood brings peace. And in those times, when peace between you and another is not possible, look to Jesus and release your angst to Him. Let His peace rule in your heart and be thankful (1 Corinthians 6:7, Colossians 3:15).

> *"If possible, so far as it depends on you, live peaceably with all."*
> *Romans 12:18*

Question: How does looking to Jesus and His cross put to death hostility and conflict in your life?

_____

_____

_____

_____

Looking to Jesus When Feeling Overwhelmed

*"O God, listen to my cry! Hear my prayer! From the
ends of the earth, I cry to you for help when my heart
is overwhelmed. Lead me to the towering rock of safety,
for you are my safe refuge, a fortress where my enemies
cannot reach me." Psalm 61:1-3 NIV*

Sometimes life comes at us like a tsunami wave. In spite of all our time-saving
devices and organization applications, the demands on our time, money, and
energy from family, friends, jobs, school, church, and community can leave us
feeling wrecked and drowning in need - the needs of those around us and our own.

We want to be grateful, but our burdens are distracting. We long to priori-
tize, but we end up stuck pondering which fire to put out first. We are told we
need sleep, but who can get it when crying babies, sick loved ones, urgent late-
night calls, or insomnia are our constant companions. Our friends might try
to help, but they often have their own troubles. We do our best to keep moving
forward, but feelings of inadequacy and helplessness haunt and hinder us.

In our distress, we cry out with the Psalmist, "Oh, that I had wings like a
dove! I would fly away and be at rest;" (Psalm 55:4-6) But we cannot fly away
and escape when our bank account is empty, our spouse is terminally ill, or
our child is living in rebellion. No vacation is going to change the reality of our
circumstances. A cupcake, round of golf, or a glass of wine might distract us
momentarily, but they aren't going to relieve our burdens or carry us through
our times of distress.

But, there is one thing we can do when life feels overwhelming that will
not only help us but will actually sustain us and keep us safe until our storm

passes. We can look to Jesus, who on the cross was overwhelmed with our sins, sickness, and sorrows but then overcame and rose victorious over them for us. He is the Rock, the higher ground, to which we can run and find refuge when the tsunami of life hits.

Illustration

Jesus Christ is fully God, but when He came to us, He came clothed in our humanity. He subjected Himself to all the stresses and pains and trials of life that we experience.

Jesus grew up from infancy and endured family life with parents and siblings who did not understand Him (Luke 2:48-50). He suffered the disrespect and jeering of those who watched Him grow up (Matthew 13:57). When His ministry began, His family, friends, followers, and enemies pushed and prodded Him: "Give us more bread, Jesus!" "Heal my friend, Jesus!" "Save us, Jesus!" "Bless my child, Jesus!" "Answer this question, Jesus." And while all these demands wearied Him, He found rest and renewal in time alone with His Father (Luke 5:16).

But eventually, the appointed time came where there would be no respite for Jesus. Take a moment to contemplate how Jesus, the Man, was entirely overwhelmed, starting at the Garden of Gethsemane:

> *"They went to a place called Gethsemane, and Jesus said to his disciples, "Sit here while I pray." He took Peter, James, and John along with him, and he began to be deeply distressed and troubled. "My soul is overwhelmed with sorrow to the point of death," he said to them. "Stay here and keep watch." Mark 14:32-34 (NIV)*

Notice the words *"deeply distressed,"* *"troubled,"* and *"overwhelmed."* Think of what Jesus was about to endure; desertion by all His disciples, rejection by the Jewish leaders, false charges by the Jewish nation, judgment by the ruling nation, beatings and scourging by Roman soldiers, the hatred and animosity of Satan, and most importantly, the terrible wrath of His Father against sin.

Jesus was, as the ark in Noah's day, buffeted on all sides, Satan erupting up from below like the great volcanoes of the deep and God's wrath raining down like the fire and brimstone that destroyed Sodom and Gomorrah. He was deeply distressed and greatly troubled, His very soul, His inner being was truly overwhelmed in every way. So much so that His sweat became like drops of blood:

> *"And being in anguish, he prayed more earnestly, and his sweat was like drops of blood falling to the ground." Luke 22:44 (NIV)*

Jesus knew what it was like to be completely overwhelmed, and Jesus knows how to help us when we feel overwhelmed by our circumstances. He is the Rock that David praises as His Fortress, Deliverer, Savior, Refuge, Shield, Salvations, Stronghold, and Rescuer (Psalm 18:1-48, Psalm 55:16-18, Psalm 62:1). He is the constant stabilizer in your changing storm. He died for you on Calvary; He will not lose you to the waves. He will hold you fast! Look to Jesus just now.

Application

Do you feel like life is just too much? Are the demands on your time and energy draining and discouraging you? Does it seem that so many people have touched and taken from you that there is nothing left? Are you exhausted from trying to rescue others when you are already sinking beneath the burdens of your life?

Look to Jesus and see His heart crushed and distressed to bring you comfort (2 Corinthians 1:4). See Him sweating drops of blood to bring you peace (John 14:17). See Him cursed and mocked so that you might be blessed and affirmed (Ephesians 1:3). See Him pouring out His life to provide you with sustaining grace (Hebrews 1:3).

Consider the fire of God's wrath poured out on Jesus so that there would be no condemnation for you regardless of how you perform under pressure (Romans 8:1). You have been rescued, dear friend; you are safe in Jesus! No storm of this life can consume you because you have been purchased with the precious blood of Jesus (1 Peter 1:18-19). Jesus is Yours, and you are His (Song of Solomon 6:3)

When you feel life is suffocating you, think of how Jesus hung on the cross gasping for air and then how He breathed His last so that you would be filled and empowered by His Spirit (Romans 8:10-11). Because of Jesus' sacrifice, when you look to Him, you are able to not only survive but also supernaturally rise above the chaos that surrounds and threatens you (Philippians 1:12-18).

When you have nothing to give, turn to the One that gave all and receive everything you need (2 Peter 1:3). Jesus sacrificed His life to save and sanctify you (John 3:16, Hebrews 10:10). Believe in Him, trust in Him! He is the Resurrection and the Life (John 11:25). Oh, friend, behold the Lamb of God that not only takes away your sin but also transforms you into His image (2 Corinthians 3:18).

When you feel overwhelmed by life, don't escape into social media, try to reform yourself with a new program, or attempt to life-hack your brain into thinking everything is really fine. Instead, look to Jesus, the Rock that is higher and greater, the Rock struck for you. Every blow that He took from fist or hammer was for you; He was torn down to build you up (John 2:19, Acts 20:32).

Come now and pour out your heart to Jesus; He is waiting to receive you, ready to lift you and tell you great and unsearchable things that you would not have known apart from this moment (Jeremiah 33:3, John 14:12-14). He has redeemed you; He will carry you through your time of difficulty safely.

> *"Fear not, for I have redeemed you; I have called you by name; you are mine. When you pass through the waters, I will be with you; and through the rivers, they shall not overwhelm you; when you walk through fire you shall not be burned, and the flame shall not consume you. For I am the Lord your God, the Holy One of Israel, your Savior..." Isaiah 43:1-3*

Question: How does considering Christ's overwhelming experience in the Garden of Gethsemane and on the cross give you hope when you are feeling overwhelmed by the circumstances of life?

DAY 30:

Looking to Jesus When Facing Death

*"Since the children have flesh and blood, he too shared
in their humanity so that by his death he might break
the power of him who holds the power of death—that is,
the devil—and free those who all their lives were held
in slavery by their fear of death." Hebrews 2:14-15 NIV*

*P*hysical death is an equalizer because it is no respecter of persons. Death
does not see age, gender, race, or faith. It cares not for money or status.
It is merely a part of the current order of things. We live until we die. But the
certainty of death does not make it a welcome or desirable reality.

Every day around the world, we fight to live. Some efforts are small: we
maneuver carefully, take precautions, test for safety, warn of danger, follow
exercise regimes, consider our diet, etc. Some efforts are extreme: amputations,
transplants, experimental therapies, and more. And generally speaking, our
life-saving efforts are appropriate. God has given us the gift of life; it would be
foolish to treat it as trivial and inconsequential.

But what do we do when we feel death's proximity increasing in our lives?
Are we without recourse when accidents, disease, and calamity strike? As those
who have been raised to a new life in Christ, can we face the end of our life or
watch the life of someone we love ebb away with faith instead of fear?

Oh, dear friend, we cannot escape the sadness of loss, but we can indeed face
our death or grieve our loved ones *with hope* as those who have already died
with Christ and risen to a new life in Him (1 Thessalonians 4:14, Romans 6:4-8).

When death stops being an inevitability and becomes your reality, you have
a safe haven in your Lord Jesus Christ! Fear and sorrow cannot consume you

when you are filled with Jesus, Your eternal Life. In your time of need, you can look to Jesus and find comfort in His Calvary love knowing that at the end of this life, you will not see death, but Christ, who is your life (John 8:51)!

> *"If then you have been raised with Christ, seek the things that are above, where Christ is, seated at the right hand of God. Set your minds on things that are above, not on things that are on earth. For you have died, and your life is hidden with Christ in God. When Christ who is your life appears, then you also will appear with him in glory." Colossians 3:1-4*

Illustration

In the Old Testament book of 1 Samuel, we learn that one of Israel's greatest kings, David, was a shepherd before he became the King of Israel. One day, during those early shepherding years of his life, David was sent by his father to check on his brothers who were serving in Israel's army. And when David arrived at Israel's encampment, he saw a giant named Goliath mocking the armies of God. David was appalled at the giant's mockery of God, so David volunteered to fight the giant.

God had prepared David by having David fight and overcome a lion and a bear in his role as a shepherd. David's battle with Goliath was short-lived because David knocked Goliath out with a single stone thrown from his slingshot. David then grabbed the giant's own weapon, a massive sword, and cut off Goliath's head with it. With this single act of victory, David ended Goliath's life and empowered God's people to overcome their enemy, the Philistines (1 Samuel 17:51-53).

Similarly, Jesus, our Shepherd from Bethlehem, was sent by His Father on a mission of mercy to us, His brothers and sisters. While here, Jesus took Satan's own weapon, death, and used it to defeat Satan and remove Satan's power over us. Jesus' death on the cross set us free from the fear of death and empowered us with His eternal life. Jesus destroyed death; you are free from it (Hebrews 2:14-15). Jesus has given you His Spirit to be with you always to comfort and encourage you all the way to glory.

"Death has been swallowed up in victory." "Where, O death, is your victory? Where, O death, is your sting?" 1 Corinthians 15:54-55

The bee of death stung Jesus and died, so now death can never sting any believer. You have nothing to fear with death! Jesus died and rose again to *"free those who all their lives were held in slavery by their fear of death."* (Hebrews 2:14-15 NIV) When we Christians depart this world, we leave as victors returning to our Lord and King (2 Corinthians 5:8, 1 Timothy 1:17).

Application

Have you gotten the news that you or someone you love has a terminal disease? In your grief, look to Jesus. As you navigate the journey ahead, call out to the One who has died your death and delivered you from the fear of what lies ahead (Psalm 18:28-36, Psalm 130:1-8).

Jesus loves you; He will carry you and those you love through this time of suffering (Isaiah 40:11). We might be frightened by disease and death, but when we look to Jesus, we see Him standing up for us, saying, *"Fear not, I am the first and the last, and the living one. I died, and behold I am alive forevermore..."* (Revelation 1:17-18).

Has someone you love died unexpectedly? Miscarriages, stillbirths, infant deaths, accidents, homicides, aneurysms, heart attacks, embolisms, and so much more take our loved ones from us suddenly every day. It is shocking and hard to accept such dramatic losses, but we can find comfort and courage in the gospel of Jesus Christ.

To comfort and encourage the Thessalonians believers who were grieving the loss of their loved ones, Paul wrote, *"For since we believe that Jesus died and rose again, even so, through Jesus, God will bring with him those who have fallen asleep."* (1 Thessalonians 4:14). Jesus has defeated death, and all who "fall asleep" in Him are escorted into eternity by their Bridegroom of eternal love and life. Speak this message of hope in Jesus' death and resurrection to your heart, friend, and encourage others with it.

Grieving is hard, perplexing, and distressing work, but if we carry in our hearts and minds the death of Christ, then we will experience and see His resurrection life manifested in us. On the cross, Jesus was crushed and destroyed so that you would be made whole and held secure for eternity. Jesus intimately knows your grief; He will see you through it.

Look to Jesus now. See that He lowered Himself all the way to death on a criminal's cross to lift you, dear believer, higher. He has taken you out of the kingdom of death and seated you in heavenly places. Death and sorrow cannot defeat you because Jesus has overcome them for you. Look to Jesus and allow His sacrificial love to comfort you and carry you through your time of loss.

> *"For God did not appoint us to suffer wrath but to receive salvation through our Lord Jesus Christ. 10 He died for us so that, whether we are awake or asleep, we may live together with him" (1 Thessalonians 5:9-10).*

Question: How does looking to Jesus' atoning death on the cross and His victorious resurrection encourage your heart when thinking of physical death?

Made in the USA
Monee, IL
25 March 2021

63702374R10077